Sensational life

An Interactive Guide

W PUBLISHING GROUP™

www.wpublishinggroup.com

A Division of Thomas Nelson, Inc.
www.ThomasNelson.com

SENSATIONAL LIFE: AN INTERACTIVE GUIDE

© 2003 W Publishing Group. All rights reserved. No portion of this book may be reproduced, stored in a retrieval system, or transmitted in any form or by any means—electronic, mechanical, photocopy, recording, or any other—except for brief quotations in printed reviews, without the prior permission of the publisher.

Published by W Publishing Group, a Division of Thomas Nelson, Inc., P.O. Box 141000, Nashville, TN 37214.

Prepared with the assistance of The Livingstone Corporation. Project staff members include Neil Wilson and Linda Taylor.

Unless otherwise indicated, Scripture quotations used in this book are from the Holy Bible, New Century Version, copyright © 1987, 1988, 1991 by Word Publishing, Dallas, Texas 75234. Used by permission.

Other Scripture references are from the following sources:

The Living Bible (TLB), copyright © 1971 by Tyndale House Publishers, Wheaton, Ill. Used by permission.

The Message (MSG), copyright © 1993. Used by permission of NavPress Publishing Group.

New American Standard Bible (NASB), © 1960, 1977, by the Lockman Foundation.

The Holy Bible, New International Version (NIV). Copyright © 1973, 1978, 1984, International Bible Society. Used by permission of Zondervan Bible Publishers.

The Holy Bible, New Living Translation (NLT), copyright © 1996 by Tyndale House Publishers, Wheaton, Illinois. Used by permission.

The New King James Version (NKJV®), copyright 1979, 1980, 1982, Thomas Nelson, Inc., Publishers.

The New Revised Standard Version Bible (NRSV), © 1989 by the Division of Christian Education of the National Council of the Churches of Christ in the USA.

Printed in the United States of America

03 04 05 06 PHX 9 8 7 6 5 4 3 2

Contents

You Can Live a Sensational Life • v

Getting the Most from Your Sensational Life Conference Experience • vi

SESSION 1: **Introduction** • 1
Living a Sensational Life: Welcoming Vignettes from Patsy, Sheila, Marilyn, Thelma, and Luci

SESSION 2: **Vision in a Sensational Life** • 3
Sheila Walsh: Join the Race!

SESSION 3: **Truth in a Sensational Life** • 19
Patsy Clairmont: Life Maps and "Mo" Moments

SESSION 4: **Peace in a Sensational Life** • 35
Thelma Wells: Be Anxious for Nothing

SESSION 5: **Endurance in a Sensational Life** • 51
Barbara Johnson: Just Another Hurdle in the Road

SESSION 6: **Wholeness in a Sensational Life** • 63
Marilyn Meberg: Gun It!

SESSION 7: **Celebration in a Sensational Life** • 81
Luci Swindoll: The Real Reason to Celebrate

SESSION 8: **Wrap-Up** • 95
Sheila Walsh: Sensational Little Gifts to Take Home

You Can Live a Sensational Life

The thief comes only to steal and kill and destroy. I came that they may have life, and have it abundantly.
—John 10:10 (NRSV)

The opportunities for living a sensational life are all around you—no matter what circumstances you find yourself in right now. In these eight laughter-filled, honestly shared, soul-searching sessions led by six dynamic speakers—Sheila Walsh, Patsy Clairmont, Thelma Wells, Barbara Johnson, Marilyn Meberg, and Luci Swindoll—you will discover how to make every day you live sensational. The discovery evolves as you recognize that you serve a sensational Savior who desires to give you an abundant life overflowing with vision, truth, peace, endurance, wholeness, and celebration.

Sharing insights you may never have considered before, these lively speakers will show you that your life doesn't have to be out of the ordinary to be sensational; it needs only to be grounded in the will of God and lived for his glory. Then you will find that Jesus does indeed give life, and he gives it "abundantly."

Getting the Most from Your Sensational Life Conference Experience

The Women of Faith Sensational Life conference features six outstanding speakers who offer their perspectives on how you can live a sensational life. This interactive guide has been designed to help you enjoy, remember, reflect on, and apply the wisdom and lessons shared by these six experienced sisters in Christ.

We've organized the materials into a series of eight sessions, but of course you can use the videos and workbook any way you choose. You may enjoy using these materials on your own as a richly rewarding daily devotional. If so, you have the freedom to choose your own scheduling and timing preferences.

If you're sharing the Sensational Life conference experience with others, we've included two lesson-plan formats for each session to assist groups both large and small. The formats are explained below; choose the one that works best for your allotted time and setting.

Promoting Your Gatherings

Showing the twelve-minute Introductions and Welcoming Vignettes on Tape 1 is a great way to promote your upcoming Women of Faith Sensational Life conference experience. The insightful and funny vignettes give potential participants an idea of the format and content of the Sensational Life conference. It also encourages them to register and get the interactive guide books so they can participate.

Choosing a Group Format and Planning the Sessions

Sensational Life: An Interactive Guide offers two outlined formats for use with small or large groups. If you have ninety minutes or more to devote to each session, you can use the Full-Length Option. If you only have sixty minutes to spend per session, the Fast-Track Option will probably work best for you. The first difference in the two options is that the Full-Length Option includes showing each speaker's two-minute Welcoming Vignette before showing her main presentation (or having a participant read aloud the vignette script); on the Fast-Track Option, participants are asked to read the script before the session begins so that your time together jumps right to the main presentation. The other difference in the two options is that the Full-Length Option allows time for discussing the Back-Stage Pass Bible Studies as a group. If you follow the shorter Fast-Track Option, you or your group members should use the Bible studies as a means of reviewing the topics between sessions.

Because these video presentations were originally taped during a weekend Women of Faith conference, they also make an excellent series for a Friday-night/all-day-Saturday schedule such as a women's retreat, a weekend church-women's conference, or similar gathering.

Managing Your Time

If you're using the videos and workbook in a group setting, we suggest you stick to the proposed schedule as much as possible. Gently encourage the women to participate and express their thoughts, but ask them to keep their remarks brief. Don't let discussions wander off-topic. Group gatherings—especially gatherings of women who may have family, work, or schooling commitments—are most successful when participants can depend on every session beginning and ending on time. Each session outline includes a time line for both the Full-Length and Fast-Track Options suggesting the time to be allotted for each part of the session.

In case you're adapting the videos for your own customized schedule, the following list shows you the time required for the main video segment corresponding to each session. Remember that you may also choose to play each speaker's two-minute Welcoming Vignette on Tape 1 during her session before continuing on to her main video presentation. The thought-provoking lesson plans for each of the sessions will guide you in using the rest of your allotted time to discuss and apply the speaker's message.

> Session 1—Introduction and Welcoming Vignettes (12 minutes)
> Session 2—Sheila Walsh (30 minutes)
> Session 3—Patsy Clairmont (40 minutes)
> Session 4—Thelma Wells (30 minutes)
> Session 5—Barbara Johnson (10 minutes)
> Session 6—Marilyn Meberg (40 minutes)
> Session 7—Luci Swindoll (35 minutes)
> Session 8—Wrap-Up (13 minutes)

Using the Interactive Guide and Videos

Whether you follow the Full-Length or the Fast-Track Option or choose to develop your own time line, each session is designed to reveal to you the rich, rewarding blessings of the sensational life God calls his followers to live. While the Introduction and Wrap-Up Sessions are less structured, the six main sessions, on both the Full-Length and Fast-Track Options, are divided into the following segments:

Leader's Notes. These self-explanatory notes are included throughout the workbook for group leaders who are facilitating discussions during the sessions. Participants in groups can also review these guidelines to gain a sense of where the facilitator might direct the discussion. These notes, however, are merely suggestions.

Introductions, Welcome, and Prayer. Women of Faith conferences are well known for the camaraderie they create. We've intentionally left this part of the session outline unscripted so that your gathering can begin as a warm, informal gathering of friends. As each session begins, the leader should introduce herself and then ask participants to introduce (or reintroduce) themselves. For variety, or as an "icebreaker," ask each woman to say her name and tell one new thing about herself ("I have six children" or "I grew up in Alaska" or "I collect old Bibles"). If the group is auditorium-sized, ask each woman to do the same with the four women to her right and left and in front and back of her (always remind everyone to be brief—this is an introduction time, not a discussion session!).

The leader should then briefly summarize that you're following *Sensational Life: An Interactive Guide,* reminding the women that last week you heard _____ speak on _____, and during this session you'll be listening to and discussing _____'s presentation on _____. For example, the leader might say, "Last week we enjoyed Sheila's presentation on vision in a sensational life. This morning we'll be hearing and discussing Patsy Clairmont's perspective on truth in a sensational life."

Setting the Stage. At the beginning of the Women of Faith conference, five of the speakers present a two-minute Welcoming Vignette that evokes laughter and delivers memorable insights. These vignettes are so revealing of each speaker's lifestyle and personality that we include the vignette scripts here at the beginning of each speaker's workbook session. If you've chosen the Full-Length Option, we suggest you replay each speaker's Welcoming Vignette from Tape 1 during that session's Setting the Stage segment (or have someone read aloud the script). If you're following the Fast-Track Option, you will skip the Welcoming Vignette videos, so you should read the vignette transcript, printed in the Setting the Stage segment, *before* the session so you can go directly to the Main Event. The exception to this is Barbara Johnson's presentation in Session 5. Due to health problems, Barbara's involvement in the Sensational Life conference was limited, and she did not appear in the Welcoming Vignettes. So in Session 5 you will watch Barbara's main video presentation and have extra time for discussing her topic afterward.

Main Event. These speakers are on a mission, and they don't dillydally around as they're laying out their battle plans! This section of the workbook, with its fill-in-the-blank highlights taken from each speaker's talk, is designed to make note taking simple. We suggest that you scan through each session's Main Event section before viewing the videotape so you'll know what to listen for. Then, as you watch the presentation, you'll be prepared to fill in the blanks and keep track of the speaker's main points as she takes you through her perspective of sensational living.

Taking It to Heart. There's a fine line between laughter and tears, and you'll find that the line often gets erased during these sessions. Part of the benefit of watching and listening to these women comes from the experience itself. They're good company! They're the kind of friends who lift your spirits by their very presence. Their words remind you that others share your experiences and thoughts as a woman and that, contrary to what you may sometimes feel, you really are not alone. It's encouraging to know that others have walked the same path and have lived to talk about it. You can benefit from their stories.

Be careful not to rush through the Taking It to Heart sections. These spaces and questions will allow you to record your feelings and thoughts while the session lessons are fresh in your mind. Consider the questions carefully and be honest in your answers.

If you are working through this study with a group, you will have a rich opportunity to add your own story to the encouragement offered by the conference speakers. If necessary, organize yourselves into small groups to briefly share your thoughts with each other, remembering that you may find someone in your group has just as much to teach you as the amazing women on the screen. God has a wonderful way of putting kindred hearts in front of us, one way or another!

Taking It Home. Now comes the hard part—application. Women of Faith has a mission statement that begins,

> Women of Faith's mission is to see women set
> free to a lifestyle of God's truth and grace.

These women and the organization they represent hope to impact your life for the better. That's how the effectiveness of this experience will ultimately be measured: by the way it changes you. As you enjoy this conference experience, we hope your view of God and of yourself, your attitude toward the world around you, and the way you live will all begin to reflect what Jesus came to give—abundant, sensational life! Use the questions in the Taking It Home section to apply the lessons in the session to yourself and to work out your life plan in the context of living a sensational life.

Back-Stage Pass—Bible Studies. Each of these six speakers has spoken from the thoughts hidden in her heart combined with lessons from God's Word. Behind each story and idea these women share, you will find a deep desire to communicate the truth from Scripture.

This section offers Bible studies that take you into the passages to which the speakers referred, along with other relevant statements from Scripture. The material is designed to help you learn the lessons they shared as well as to hide them in your heart. Depending on whether you're following the Full-Length or Fast-Track Option, you may complete these Bible studies in your group during the session or on your own as a means of reviewing between sessions. The exception to the time-line schedule again comes in Session 5. Because of the brevity of Barbara Johnson's Main Event segment, you should have time to complete at least one of the Session 5 Back-Stage Pass segments as a group.

Everyone has her own preferred translation of the Bible, and we hope you'll bring yours to each session and use it to study the highlighted passages. In case it's more convenient for you, though, we've included most of the passages in the session plans. You may find that the Bible passages quoted by the speakers differ from those translations printed here or from your own favorite translation, but you will be able to follow their teaching without a problem. Many times it enhances a Bible study to observe how the different Bible versions translate a particular passage.

A Last Word and Closing Prayer. Each session ends with a final thought to share before closing your Sensational Life experience with prayer. This section highlights at least one central, memorable insight from the speaker's presentation. Think about the closing thought presented here as an idea to ponder during the coming week.

Here We Go!

Jesus promised abundant life—but you wouldn't know it from the way many of us live. Too many Christians are just as bogged down as everyone else in the world! That's not God's way. Of course, God never promised that our lives would be easy; in fact, we can count on facing difficulty and suffering during our lives. However, as believers, our responses to these situations should be much different from what we see in the rest of the world. Why? Because we have a sensational Savior who promises to walk with us every step of the way, who already knows our earthly lives from beginning to end (no situation we face ever takes *him* by surprise), and who promises to work all things together for our good.

Are you ready to add a new, vibrant dimension to your daily walk? Then let's get started. It's time to begin our study of how to live a sensational life!

> SESSION 1

INTRODUCTION

Living a Sensational Life: Welcoming Vignettes from Patsy, Sheila, Marilyn, Thelma, and Luci

> **Leader's NOTES**

This session is intentionally unscripted so that the members of your group can spend informal time getting acquainted.

Open the session with a warm welcome then lead the group in prayer, asking God to prepare your hearts and minds for the journey you're undertaking. Take a moment to have someone read aloud the key verse for the conference and the "You Can Live a Sensational Life" introduction on page v. Then view the twelve-minute introductory tape that begins the conference and includes the Introduction by Mary Graham (the emcee) and the Welcoming Vignettes by the speakers. Stop the tape after Luci Swindoll's vignette.

Use the remainder of the time to get to know each other. Go around the room or the table (or divide an auditorium-sized gathering into small groups of four to six women), inviting each participant to introduce herself and share one fact about herself she would like the others to know (for example, where she lives or works, her favorite hobby, or the title of the last book she read). When the hubbub has quieted, invite the participants to share other brief glimpses into their lives, suggesting one or more of the following get-acquainted topics:

1. Invite the women to briefly talk about why they have chosen to participate in this conference experience and what needs they hope it will fill in their lives.

2. Ask them to express what "sensational living" means to them now, as the series begins. We'll ask this question again later, in the Wrap-Up Session at the end.

3. Use the speakers' Welcoming Vignettes as a springboard for brief discussion. Ask that each woman say which one of the Welcoming Vignettes applied most personally to her. Who, like Patsy, sometimes finds the truth hard to swallow? Who feels like Sheila—life is fine . . . until you get out of bed each morning? Who identifies with Marilyn—suffering with misconceptions because life hasn't turned out as you expected? Who understands Thelma's feelings—searching in the wrong places for peace? Who shares Luci's motto touting "spontaneous celebrations"? Talk about the vignettes and use them as a way to get to know one another better.

Preparing for Next Time. Read through Session 2 in the workbook before the next meeting, and don't forget to bring your Bible. If you're following the Fast-Track Option, it's especially important, before the next session, to read the script of Sheila's Welcoming Vignette in the Setting the Stage segment, as this video will not be shown during your session.

> SESSION 2

VISION IN A SENSATIONAL LIFE

SHEILA WALSH: Join the Race!

Full-Length Option (90 minutes)

Introductions, Welcome, and Opening Prayer (5 minutes)

Setting the Stage (2 minutes to view Sheila's Welcoming Vignette on Tape 1—or to have someone read the vignette script aloud)

Main Event (Tape 1—30 minutes)

Taking It to Heart (15 minutes)

Taking It Home (20 minutes)

Back-Stage Pass—Bible Studies (15 minutes)

A Last Word and Closing Prayer (3 minutes)

Fast-Track Option (60 minutes)

Introductions, Welcome, and Opening Prayer (5 minutes)

Setting the Stage (Read the Welcoming Vignette script on your own before the session begins.)

Main Event (Tape 1—30 minutes)

Taking It to Heart (10 minutes)

Taking It Home (10 minutes)

Back-Stage Pass—Bible Studies (Complete these Bible studies later at your convenience.)

A Last Word and Closing Prayer (5 minutes)

Setting the Stage

> ## Leader's NOTES

If you're following the Fast-Track Option, skip now to the Main Event. If you're following the Full-Length Option, have Tape 1 cued to Sheila's Welcoming Vignette (note that she is the second person to give her welcome, after Patsy Clairmont). Play the vignette during the Setting the Stage segment. At the end of the vignette, fast-forward the tape so it's ready to play Sheila's main presentation. Or, if this fast-forwarding procedure is awkward for you, cue the tape to Sheila's main presentation and ask a member of the group to read aloud the script of "The Great Mistake of Getting Up" now.

Through the two-minute Welcoming Vignettes, each of the Women of Faith speakers introduces herself with a revealing glimpse into her style, thinking, and sense of humor. Sheila Walsh's Welcoming Vignette shares an e-mail from a friend that, she says, encapsulates her life.

Sheila's Welcoming Vignette: The Great Mistake of Getting Up

One of my friends sent something in the mail to me the other day. I loved it when I read it, and I thought, *This is my life.*

It says, "Dear Lord, I have not gossiped, lost my temper, been greedy, grumpy, nasty, selfish, or self-indulgent. I have not whined, complained, cursed, or eaten any chocolate. I have charged nothing on my credit card . . . But I will be getting out of bed in a minute, and I think I'll really need your help then."

Yep . . . I do fine until I make that great mistake every morning of getting up.

SENSATIONAL LIFE

I have the privilege of talking to you about vision in a sensational life. I know what you're thinking: *Vision? I'm too busy to get my nails done; don't talk to me about vision.* But I believe that Jesus is going to meet with us here and renew vision for those who have lost it. And if you've never had a vision for your life, I believe that Jesus will give you a vision and a passion for life that's not just for a few special people; it's for every single person because, to Jesus, we are his kids, and he wants to give us a vision for a sensational life.

Main Event

Leader's **NOTES**

When you preview the video, fill out this section yourself so you can anticipate some of the participants' responses to Sheila's message. This preparation will also give you an idea of how much time you should allow at the end of the video for the women to finish making notes. Remember to have your group take a moment to read through the Main Event section before viewing the video so everyone's ready to fill in the blanks and jot down notes as the video is shown.

Video Presentation by Sheila Walsh:
Absolute Surrender, Unflagging Devotion

Sheila begins her presentation by singing the hymn "Be Thou My Vision" (not included on the video). Then she continues with her talk.

He loved the words of that hymn. He'd learned them when he was just a young boy growing up in Scotland. They were buried deep in the recesses of his heart so that no matter where he went, they were always present in the fabric of his life. Whether it was in 1924 when he was running in the Olympic Games in Paris, representing the United

Kingdom, or whether it was now, 1945, when he was being held in a Japanese prisoner of war camp. He and his sister, Jenny, were missionaries to China, and now they found themselves in a prisoner of war camp. The man was Eric Liddell. If you've ever seen the movie *Chariots of Fire,* that tells a part of Eric's story, but there's so much more. He lived his whole life as a race. He lived his whole life knowing where he was going. He lived his whole life running to God.

And then, when he was just forty-three years old, he died. They held a small ceremony for him in the prisoner of war camp and invited anyone who wanted to, to come and take part and pay respects to this amazing man. The pastor who was leading the simple service said, "Is there anyone who would like to say a few words?"

A young woman stepped forward. People were surprised to even see her there, much less attempting to say something. Everyone knew who she was. She was the camp prostitute. She stepped forward and said, "Eric Liddell knew that I needed to have a shelf put up in my hut. And he went in, and he put that shelf up for me. He was the first man in my life who did something for me and didn't want anything in return." She stepped back into the crowd.

A young man, eighteen years old, stepped forward. He was holding a pair of running shoes. He said, "Last winter, Eric Liddell looked down at my feet and discovered that I didn't have any shoes on. He gave me what had to be his prized possession. He gave me his running shoes." The young man stepped back into the crowd.

The pastor who was leading the service asked everyone who was present there at the gravesite this question: "What was the secret of his consecrated life and influence? Absolute surrender to the will of God and a devotion that never flagged." . . .

Absolute surrender to the will of God and a devotion that never flagged—whether he was running in the Olympic Games or whether he was walking through a prisoner of war camp.

The two secrets to Eric Liddell's consecrated life are so important, Sheila repeated them:
1. Absolute _____ to the will of God.
2. A _____ that never flagged.

If I were to sit with you tonight . . . and if I asked you, "What is the vision you have for your life?" I wonder what you would say. . . . You might think that I mean a game plan—like, "Where do you think you'll be two years from now, or how many pounds do you want to lose by August?" That's not what I'm talking about—not at all. (Sheila)

Sheila says having a vision for your life means a _____ _____ sense of _____, of knowing absolutely _____ you are on this earth and _____ you are going. It's a passion and a vision that _____ you in all the moments of your life—whether you're winning a _____ or whether you find yourself in some sort of _____.

As she considers the theme of "joining the race," Sheila explains that she has divided her talk into three parts using the story of Eric Liddell's life:

1. _____
2. _____
3. _____

Running

To the mother who wanted to begin to "do something for God," Sheila responded, "I can't think of anything more wonderful than to _____ _____ _____ to know and to love _____. I'm sure that would be the greatest _____ you could offer him."

According to Sheila, too many of us think of full-time Christian service as being _____ from our everyday lives. Instead, she points out, full-time Christian service is _____ of our lives.

> *A life lived listening to the decisive call of God is a life lived before one audience that trumps all others—the Audience of One.*
> —Os Guinness[1]

Eric Liddell's sister tried to dissuade him from running in the Olympic Games before they went to China to serve as missionaries. She told him, "God has made you for a purpose." Eric replied, "He made me for a purpose, but he also made me _____, and when I run, I feel his _____."

Sheila said, "I love that it wasn't just when [Eric Liddell] was conducting a service in a Japanese prisoner of war camp that he felt God's pleasure. It was when he was using every single gift he had."

Sheila says that every person has gifts God wants to use—and God is pleased when we use them. To the woman who feels that she could start "running her race" by hosting a small Bible study in her home, Sheila says, "____ ____!"

Fill in the blanks from Sheila's statements: Whatever you do for God is _____ to him. Your _____ _____ can be an act of _____. God doesn't _____ a single thing you do. God misses _____.

To the woman who wanted to become a writer, Sheila said, "____ __ ____."

Do you want to do something for God? Sheila says simply, "_____." Put your running shoes on, remember you're running to _____, and _____ the race.

Falling

Sheila describes the person who has "fallen" on the track this way: "Even though you're sitting in your seat, internally you're lying on the track, _____ and _____, facedown."

The questions that often trip us up on the track of life are the _____ questions.

Sheila says the _____ questions are very much a part of the race. When you get back up again, you are not the _____. You don't run the same way. There's a new _____, _____, and _____ because you know who you are running to.

Are you going to understand everything this side of heaven? Circle one: Yes   No

What can you do when you've fallen and you lie on the track with your questions?
   1. You lift your _____ _____.
   2. You remember _____ _____ _____ ____.

3. You look at _____.
4. You get back on the _____.
5. You keep on _____.

Jesus, who is our example, never lost sight of _____ ____ _____ _____.

When pain crowds your heart and mind so much that it's all you can see, look _____ and remember _____ you're running.

Finishing

Sometimes we want to quit. Like Sheila's son, you might feel like it's too _____ and there's far too much _____ _____.

Sheila shared about her struggles in dealing with clinical depression. Then, she said, psychiatrists helped her understand that "just as there are those who wear glasses to correct an imperfection in _____, there also is a way to correct an imperfection in the _____ chemicals in your _____."

Jesus met me in the midst of that dark place and ran beside me.
—*Sheila*

Recently, when Sheila's doctor called, she was doodling on a scratch pad, considering whether she should change her hairstyle. After the doctor said she might have cancer, Sheila looked at the hairstyle sketches on her scratchpad and prayed, "God, just _____ ___ _____. Just give me a _____."

After Sheila's diagnosis came back she felt a mixture of two feelings:

1. _____
2. _____

She had those feelings because she realized that at any moment in our life—one phone call or a letter can come in, and it _____ _____.

When that one moment comes that changes your life, how can you finish the race when everything in you is aching? Sheila turned to Scripture and found comfort and encouragement in Hebrews 12: "Keep your _____ on Jesus, who both _____ and _____ this race we're in. Study how he did it. Because he never lost sight of _____ _____ _____ _____." (MSG).

Sheila concluded, "The wonderful thing about this race we are in is that we are not _____. _____ is with you; in all the moments of your life _____ to _____."

Taking It to Heart
Questions to help you personalize the lessons in the session

> ### Leader's NOTES
>
> Give the group a few moments to work on these questions silently before you invite sharing. Since the women may not know each other well yet, be sensitive in how strongly you encourage them to share at this point. They may not be ready to join the race just yet!

1. Where are you on the "track of life"? Circle one.
   A. I'd like to be in on the running; I just need the courage to put on my shoes.
   B. I'm in pretty bad shape right now. I've fallen, and I'm not sure how to get up.
   C. I feel like quitting. I just don't think I can take it anymore.

2. Sheila asked, "I wonder how you feel about your life. Did it work out how you thought it would? Are you living the life you imagined? Or are you lost somewhere?" Answer and explain.

3. Look at your daily routine and consider what will help you see all that you do each day as part of your "full-time Christian service." How can you sense God's pleasure in all that you do?

Taking It Home
Questions to help you apply the lessons from the session

◉ Leader's **NOTES**

Sheila's presentation covered a range of emotions as she discussed a woman's need to get in on the race, no matter what their current stage in life. Those who want to run may just need the courage to put on their shoes and *do it*. Others have fallen on the track, dealing with severe difficulties or crises. Still others may just want to quit. You may have representatives of each of these areas in your own group. The most difficult part of your role as leader is to know when to stick with the script and when to expand on the group's responses. By the time you get to this point in the session, the group may have discovered its own pace and needs.

It's probably more important in the long run that the women get their needs heard and responded to than that the lesson be completely "filled out." Just be careful not to let one person dominate your entire session. If the women need to be heard, tactfully make sure to give everyone a chance to talk. But be mindful of the time; your participants will appreciate your making sure the session ends on time. Encourage those who need more sharing time to stay later after the session officially ends (if this is possible in the setting where you're meeting), or suggest that they set up another time and place to continue their sharing.

1. As Sheila described Eric Liddell's life, she said that the secrets to his consecrated life were "absolute surrender" and "a devotion that never flagged." How would you picture these attitudes in your life?

   In my life, absolute surrender would look like:
   _____
   _____

   In my life, unflagging devotion would look like:
   _____
   _____

2. How would you describe your vision for your life? What are you passionate about?
   _____
   _____
   _____

3. Complete these statements:
   A. I am here on this earth to _____.
   B. I know where I am going, and that is _____.

4. What would you say to someone who wants to quit the race?
   _____
   _____
   _____

Back-Stage Pass—Bible Studies
Scripture passages used by Sheila Walsh

It is important to keep in mind that all the Women of Faith speakers are committed to basing their teaching on the Bible. Underlying their honesty and vulnerability is their genuine desire to communicate the truth from the Word of God.

⟩ Leader's NOTES

If you're following the Fast-Track Option and using the Back-Stage Pass segment as a means of reviewing between meetings, direct the women to skip now to A Last Word at the end of the session and to complete the Bible studies later, at their convenience. If your group is following the Full-Length Option, you will have fifteen minutes to work together through the following discussion of Sheila's selected Bible passages in this session. Ask one of the participants to read each passage aloud, then guide the women through the questions that follow. If time runs out, you may have to complete the Bible studies later at home. You'll have an opportunity during the Wrap-Up Session to share some of the insights you note here.

Luke 7:18–28

[18] John's followers told him about all these things. He called for two of his followers [19] and sent them to the Lord to ask, "Are you the One who is to come, or should we wait for someone else?"

[20] When the men came to Jesus, they said, "John the Baptist sent us to you with this question: 'Are you the One who is to come, or should we wait for someone else?'"

[21] At that time, Jesus healed many people of their sicknesses, diseases, and evil spirits, and he gave sight to many blind people. [22] Then Jesus answered John's followers, "Go tell John what you saw and heard here. The blind can see, the crippled can walk, and people with skin diseases are healed. The deaf can hear, the dead are raised to life, and the Good News is preached to the poor. [23] Those who do not stumble in their faith because of me are blessed!"

[24] When John's followers left, Jesus began talking to the people about John: "What did you go out into the desert to see? A reed blown by the wind? [25] What did you go out to see? A man dressed in fine clothes? No, people who have fine clothes and much wealth live in kings' palaces. [26] But what did you go out to see? A prophet? Yes, and I tell you, John is more than a prophet. [27] This was written about him: 'I will send my

messenger ahead of you, who will prepare the way for you.' ²⁸I tell you, John is greater than any other person ever born, but even the least important person in the kingdom of God is greater than John."

Luke 7:18–28 Study Questions

An introductory thought from Sheila:

> Don't you think it's significant that the last piece of dialogue in the New Testament that we have of John [the Baptist's] speaking is a question? John is in prison, he's about to be beheaded, and he says to his friends, "Will you go to Jesus and ask him, 'Are you the One, or should we expect another?'" How strange that John would ask that! He's the one who has lived his whole life preparing for the moment when he would say, "Behold the Lamb of God, who takes away the sin of the world!" He saw the Spirit descend on Jesus as a dove. But now, in his last hours on this earth, he thinks, *Did I get it wrong?*

1. What do you think could have caused John's doubt? What do you think Jesus had done (or not done) that caused John to ask this question?

   _____
   _____
   _____

2. What reply did Jesus give to John the Baptist's friends?

   _____
   _____
   _____

3. Read Isaiah 29:18–19, 35:5–6, and 61:1–2. How are these verses significant in light of Jesus' response to John?

   _____
   _____
   _____

4. What was Jesus saying about John the Baptist to the crowd in verse 27? (See also Malachi 3:1, 4:5; and Matthew 3:1–3.)

_____
_____
_____

5. Explain what you think Jesus meant in verse 28 that "John is greater than any other person" but that "even the least important person in the kingdom of God is greater than John."

_____
_____
_____

6. John doubted, but what did he do with his doubt that provides an example to you when you have doubts?

_____
_____
_____

Hebrews 12:1–3, 12–13 (MSG)

Do you see what this means—all these pioneers who blazed the way, all these veterans cheering us on? It means we'd better get on with it. Strip down, start running—and never quit! No extra spiritual fat, no parasitic sins. Keep your eyes on Jesus, who both began and finished this race we're in. Study how he did it. Because he never lost sight of where he was headed—that exhilarating finish in and with God—he could put up with anything along the way: cross, shame, whatever. And now he's there, in the place of honor, right alongside God. When you find yourselves flagging in your faith, go over that story again, item by item, that long litany of hostility he plowed through. That will shoot adrenaline into your souls! . . .

So don't sit around on your hands! No more dragging your feet! Clear the path for long-distance runners so no one will trip and fall, so no one will step in a hole and sprain an ankle. Help each other out. And run for it!

Hebrews 12:1–3, 12–13 Study Questions

1. Who do you picture in the group of "veterans" who are cheering you on in your race?
   _____
   _____
   _____

2. What comprises the "extra spiritual fat" or the "parasitic sins" that are tripping you up on the track? What do you need to do to "strip down" and run without these impediments?
   _____
   _____
   _____

3. Sheila quotes from this passage and says to "keep your eyes on Jesus" and "study how he did it." How *did* Jesus finish his race?
   _____
   _____
   _____

4. If you had been in Jesus' shoes (as a fallible human) at what points in your (his) life would you have been ready to "quit" the race?
   _____
   _____
   _____

5. Why didn't Jesus quit? What was he looking forward to?
   _____
   _____
   _____

6. What can you look forward to? Look up the following verses and fill in the blanks.

   John 14:1–3 _____

   1 Corinthians 15:51–57 _____

   1 Thessalonians 4:16–17 _____

   Revelation 21:1–6 _____

A Last Word
An insight from this session to remember until next time

> ## Leader's **NOTES**
>
> Ask someone to read Sheila's closing thought aloud before you end the session with prayer. Then invite the group members to pray for one another in the days ahead, even if the women don't know each other well yet. Remind them that we all need encouragement as we trust God to help us to join the race, get up from the track, or keep on going when we want to quit. If you're following the Fast-Track Option, briefly remind the women to complete the Back-Stage Pass Bible Studies segment from this session and also read through the Setting the Stage segment in Session 3 before your next gathering.

Closing Thought: Sheila knows that the people in her audience are in all stages of life—trying to get started in their Christian walk, trying to understand how the mundane duties of a daily life can be pleasing to God, trying to get up from the track after that one moment has occurred that changes life forever, or finding it all so hard they want to quit. Yet no matter where we find ourselves, no matter how "visionless" we may feel, we all have one thing in common. Sheila explains:

For me and for you, whether we're just putting on our shoes and tying them for the first time, whether we've fallen and we're bruised and bloodied, or whether we find ourselves asking, "Lord, how do I finish this race?" the one thing we all have to do is to look to Jesus for the way he did it. We can run to him, hide in him. . . . The wonderful thing about this race you are in is this: You are not alone. *You are not alone.* Jesus is with you. And in all the moments of your life—run, run, run . . . to him.

> SESSION 3

TRUTH IN A SENSATIONAL LIFE

PATSY CLAIRMONT:
Life Maps and "Mo" Moments

Full-Length Option (90 minutes)

Introductions, Welcome, and Opening Prayer (3 minutes)
Setting the Stage (2 minutes to review Patsy's Welcoming Vignette on Tape 1—or to have someone read the vignette script aloud)
Main Event (Tape 1—40 minutes)
Taking It to Heart (13 minutes)
Taking It Home (15 minutes)
Back-Stage Pass—Bible Studies (15 minutes)
A Last Word and Closing Prayer (2 minutes)

Fast-Track Option (60 minutes)

Introductions, Welcome, and Opening Prayer (4 minutes)
Setting the Stage (Read the Welcoming Vignette script on your own before the session begins.)
Main Event (Tape 1—40 minutes)
Taking It to Heart (7 minutes)
Taking It Home (7 minutes)
Back-Stage Pass—Bible Studies (Complete these Bible studies later at your convenience.)
A Last Word and Closing Prayer (2 minutes)

Setting the Stage

> ## Leader's NOTES

If you're following the Fast-Track Option, skip now to the Main Event. If you're following the Full-Length Option, have Tape 1 cued to Patsy's Welcoming Vignette (note that she is the first person to give her welcome). Play the vignette during the Setting the Stage segment. At the end of the vignette, fast-forward the tape so it's ready to play Patsy's main presentation. Or, if this fast-forwarding procedure is awkward for you, cue the tape to Patsy's main presentation and ask a member of the group to read aloud the script of "Truth That's Hard to Swallow" now.

Patsy's Welcoming Vignette reveals her keen sense of humor as she briefly introduces her subject of truth in a sensational life.

Patsy's Welcoming Vignette: Truth That's Hard to Swallow

Winston Churchill was regaling a group of people, except there was one person in the audience who wasn't too impressed with some things that he had said. And finally she piped up and said, "Winston Churchill, if you were my husband, I'd poison your tea."

To which he quipped back, "And madam, if you were my wife, I'd drink it."

You know, sometimes the truth is hard to swallow, if you know what I mean. We're going to talk about the aspect of truth in a sensational life. It won't be the truth that gets on your last nerve; it will be the truth that will set you free because it comes from the Word of God.

Main Event

◈ Leader's NOTES

When you preview the video, fill out this section yourself so you can anticipate some of the responses to Patsy's message. This preparation will also give you an idea of how much time you should allow at the end of the video for people to finish making notes. Remember to have your group take a moment to preview the Main Event section before viewing the video so everyone's ready to fill in the blanks and jot down notes during the video showing.

Video Presentation by Patsy Clairmont: God Uses the Strangest Folks to Get His Work Done

There was a woman who was going to go on a journey, and she decided to go by horseback. She approached the horse, she put her foot into the stirrup, grabbed hold of the horn, and slung her other leg over. But before she could settle safely into the saddle, that stallion took off at a full gallop.

She was all over that horse. She didn't have hold of the reins, she grabbed the mane, she was off to the left, she was off to the right. Pretty soon she was dangling precariously off one side. She was looking down and realized she was soon to become part of his hoofbeats if she didn't do something.

Then it came to her. "I will push off with all my might and just cast my body off to the side. I might break a few bones, but at least maybe I'll live through the experience." So she tensed up her muscles, just getting ready to push herself off . . . when Bob, the Wal-Mart greeter, came over and unplugged the horse from the wall.

Been there, done that.

Have you found that often when you go to take a trip, unexpected things happen to you?

I remember a particular journey that my husband and I were making. I had been speaking in the state of Pennsylvania. We were on the Ohio Turnpike heading for my home state of Michigan when something very unexpected—rather startling—happened. My husband was driving. We were in a conversion van, and I was on the passenger side. There was quite a bit of traffic—a lot of eighteen-wheelers—but we were moving right along through the traffic when suddenly the car door on the driver's side burst into flames. Now, I am not saying to you there was a little bit of smoke that came forth. We're talking here orange-and-red flames.

Well, I was fascinated.

Which is kind of my way of saying I was of no value in this situation at all.

I don't know if this has ever happened to you, but when you see something that makes no sense, you can't process it. It's like it erases all your brain cells. And I didn't have two left to speak to each other, so I was just sort of "observing."

My husband was far more motivated in this situation. Flames licking at his elbow as he drove, he wanted to find a solution. So he was driving with one hand, grabbed his Diet Pepsi with the other, and was trying to put the flames out while he kind of swerved over to the shoulder and was able to stop the vehicle. But when he stopped the vehicle, I leaped out. He said later that it looked like I was going to let the captain go down with the ship! But actually, when it occurred, two brain cells decided to speak. One said to the other, "Do *something*!" And that's when I thought, *Well, I'll flag down one of those eighteen-wheelers because they carry those fire extinguishers and they'll be able to put the rest of the flames out.*

Now, that was my idea. So I ran around to the back getting ready to do my three-inch great leap off the ground to flag one of these guys down when my husband yelled to me that he had doused the flames without my assistance. He invited me then to join him back in the vehicle if I chose to. I was kind of grateful that he included me in the invitation because I hadn't been a lot of help so far.

So I got back into the vehicle, and I said to Les, "You know, it was sort of like a burning bush, wasn't it?" And then I said, "But it was different than Moses' burning bush because when Moses had a burning bush, God spoke to him."

Les said, "Oh, God spoke to me, too!"

I said, "He did? What did he say?"

"He said, 'Don't count on *her* for anything!'"

Patsy says there's a lot of truth to her husband's "revelation." The problem with expecting others to rescue us, she says, is:

1. They may not have any _____ _____ on speaking terms.
2. They're not always _____ to help you or _____ to help you.
3. They may not even be in tune with the fact that ____ _____ _____.

Scripture warns us not to put our confidence in people; instead, Scripture says we should put our confidence in _____.

Moses' burning bush was unusual because, although it was burning, it was still _____. It did not turn to _____. It did not incinerate in the flames.

> *Earth is crammed with heaven, and every common bush afire with God. But only those who see take off their shoes. The rest sit round it and pluck blackberries and daub their natural faces unaware.*
> —Elizabeth Barrett Browning

When God gave Moses a life map, Moses said, in effect, "I am not _____." Patsy says, "God is the qualifier. He longs to make himself known to you in the inner person that you might gain your confidence from him and take steps into the unknown to experience the unbelievable."

> *Lord, I don't want to be unaware when you speak to me out of the commonplace! And I am so grateful that it is in commonness that your holiness is often proclaimed.*
> —*Patsy*

Patsy says we begin to understand God's plan for our lives when we find ourselves walking ___ ___ _____.

LIFE MAPS AND "MO" MOMENTS | 23

> *I love it that God uses the strangest folks to get his work done!*
>
> —Patsy

The Word of God can become a _____ for you. It can help you understand who you _____, who you are _____, and what you can _____ in him.

After she became a Christian, Patsy pictured her life map as a _____ line right up to _____.

In its next variation, her expected life map looked like _____: You _____, then you _____.

Finally, one day while she was cooking, she looked into a pot of _____ and thought, *There's my life map.*

She compares the ups and downs of her life with the travels of the Israelites described in the Bible and says, "They were all over the charts, and so will _____ be, and so will I. . . . Some seasons of our lives will seem like a _____ while others will seem like a _____ _____."

When the people were afraid by the Red Sea, they reacted to Moses with _____. They said, "Hey, Mo, . . . did you guide us out here so ___ _____ _____?"

> *Life doesn't always go smoothly. That's why I love the Israelites. They're always in some kind of mess—and I identify with that!*
>
> —Patsy

Moses' response was, "Do not _____." (See Exodus 14:13.)

He said that because he knew their _____ was coming out of their _____.

Patsy says a "Mo moment" can help you deal with sarcasm—whether it comes from others or from yourself. Say to yourself, "Honey, what are you so _____ of, that you're so bad? Are you afraid that what they just said means _____ _____ _____ _____ anymore?"

Patsy asks you to write down this verse: "The Lord will _____ for you while you _____ _____." (See Exodus 14:14.)

If you're noisy all the time, fighting your own battles, you don't give God any space to accomplish this task. We need to zip _____ _____ long enough to _____ and _____ the salvation of the Lord.

> *Often what I most need to be saved from is ME!*
> —*Patsy*

Hearing her grandson calling her "Nana" made Patsy consider how it must feel to Father God to hear his children acknowledging who he is: You are _____, and you are the One who gives _____. . . . You, Lord, are _____ _____, and we are deeply grateful.

Patsy reminds us, "Your murmuring can turn to _____ when you begin to acknowledge God."

We most need to praise God when we don't feel like _____ him. Patsy tells of a woman in constant pain who attended the conference despite her fear that the jostling of the crowds would increase her misery. Then she urges her listeners, "Be _____ to one another, dear people. You do not know the _____ the people on each side of you are bearing. . . . We don't know what's going on in their lives. We'd be much more _____ if we did."

> *Some people say that the reason the waters were sweetened by the tree is because it was a picture of a future tree, the tree of Calvary, where Jesus would die. He was the only One who could sweeten our bitter existence. It is a picture of the liberty he offers us.*
> —*Patsy*

The Israelites found water but couldn't drink it because it was so _____. God told Moses to throw a _____ into the water to sweeten it, and Moses obeyed.

Patsy says, "Whatever your landscape, the wondrous thing about our God is that he said, 'I

LIFE MAPS AND "MO" MOMENTS

_____ _____ _____ _____.' It's a sensational life, but we must plant our feet in _____ and walk in the _____ he gives. Then we will begin to see change in the dynamics because of the _____ and _____ of the Lord Jesus Christ."

Taking It to Heart
Questions to help you personalize the lessons in the session

> ## Leader's **NOTES**
>
> Give the group a few moments to work on these questions silently before you invite sharing. The level of interaction and vulnerability from the previous session may give you a good idea of how far to go in encouraging the group to share their responses to the questions.

1. Which "life map" among those that Patsy described do you most identify with? Why? (Or perhaps you have a different picture of your life map. What is it? Explain.)

   _____

   _____

2. Why do you think our lives rarely go "in a straight line right up to glory"?

   _____

   _____

"If you chart the Israelites from where they started from on their way to the Promised Land, they thought they were going to do a straight shot. Instead they were up; they were down. They were in the desert; they were on an oasis; they were on a mountaintop; they were in a valley—they were all over the charts. And so will you be, and so will I.

That's what it's like. And I think knowing the truth helps set us free from unfair expectations and resentment and disillusionment. This is what it's all about. Some seasons are more difficult than others. Some will seem like a wilderness while others will seem like a lush oasis." (Patsy)

3. How would you describe the "landscape" of your life right now? Are you on a mountaintop, in a valley, at an oasis, in the desert? Why?

_____
_____
_____

4. How can knowing the reality of these ups and downs be a "truth that sets you free" from unfair expectations, resentment, and disillusionment?

_____
_____
_____

Taking It Home
Questions to help you apply the lessons from the session

Leader's **NOTES**

Remember that it's more important in the long run that the women get their needs heard and responded to than that the lesson be completely "filled out." While discussing the following questions with your group, help the women feel free to consider the "ups and downs" of their life maps and to focus on the promise of God's presence in their lives no matter what they are going through.

1. Moses did not feel qualified to do what God called him to do. In what areas of your life do you feel "unqualified"? Why?

   _____
   _____
   _____

2. When God calls, he equips. In what ways might your lack of qualifications make you a perfect candidate for God's service? (Read 2 Corinthians 12:9.)

   _____
   _____
   _____

3. In what situations in your life do you most often find yourself "murmuring"? How can you change that murmuring to music?

   _____
   _____
   _____

4. How could you begin today to build around yourself an environment of praise to God?

   _____
   _____
   _____

Back-Stage Pass—Bible Studies
Scripture passages used by Patsy Clairmont

Like all the other Women of Faith speakers, Patsy bases her thoughts and analyzes her life experiences by the timeless truth from the Word of God.

Leader's **NOTES**

If you're following the Fast-Track Option and using the Back-Stage Pass segment as a means of reviewing between meetings, direct the women to skip now to A Last Word at the end of the session and complete the Bible studies later, at their convenience. If your group is following the Full-Length Option, ask one of the women to read each passage aloud then guide the women through the questions that follow. If time runs out, they may have to complete the Bible studies later at home. You'll have an opportunity during the Wrap-Up Session to share some of the insights noted here.

Exodus 3:1–15

¹One day Moses was taking care of Jethro's flock. (Jethro was the priest of Midian and also Moses' father-in-law.) When Moses led the flock to the west side of the desert, he came to Sinai, the mountain of God. ²There the angel of the LORD appeared to him in flames of fire coming out of a bush. Moses saw that the bush was on fire, but it was not burning up. ³So he said, "I will go closer to this strange thing. How can a bush continue burning without burning up?"

⁴When the LORD saw Moses was coming to look at the bush, God called to him from the bush, "Moses, Moses!" And Moses said, "Here I am."

⁵Then God said, "Do not come any closer. Take off your sandals, because you are standing on holy ground. ⁶I am the God of your ancestors—the God of Abraham, the God of Isaac, and the God of Jacob." Moses covered his face because he was afraid to look at God.

⁷The LORD said, "I have seen the troubles my people have suffered in Egypt, and I have heard their cries when the Egyptian slave masters hurt them. I am concerned about their pain, ⁸and I have come down to save them from the Egyptians. I will bring them out of that land and lead them to a good land with lots of room—a fertile land. It is the land of the Canaanites, Hittites, Amorites, Perizzites, Hivites, and Jebusites. ⁹I have

heard the cries of the people of Israel, and I have seen the way the Egyptians have made life hard for them. [10] So now I am sending you to the king of Egypt. Go! Bring my people, the Israelites, out of Egypt!"

[11] But Moses said to God, "I am not a great man! How can I go to the king and lead the Israelites out of Egypt?"

[12] God said, "I will be with you. This will be the proof that I am sending you: After you lead the people out of Egypt, all of you will worship me on this mountain."

[13] Moses said to God, "When I go to the Israelites, I will say to them, 'The God of your fathers sent me to you.' What if the people say, 'What is his name?' What should I tell them?"

[14] Then God said to Moses, "I AM WHO I AM. When you go to the people of Israel, tell them, 'I AM sent me to you.'"

[15] God also said to Moses, "This is what you should tell the people: 'The LORD is the God of your ancestors—the God of Abraham, the God of Isaac, and the God of Jacob. He sent me to you.' This will always be my name, by which people from now on will know me."

Exodus 3:1–15 Study Questions

1. Moses' first response to God was, "I am not a great man. How can I go to the king and lead the Israelites out of Egypt?" What other excuses did he use? (See 3:13; 4:1, 10.)

   _____
   _____
   _____

2. In Exodus 4:13, what was Moses' final excuse or dodge to avoid God's mission for his life?

   _____
   _____
   _____

3. What do you think was going through Moses' mind during this conversation with God?

   _____

4. What qualifications does it seem that Moses lacked in order to do this task?

5. On the other hand, what qualifications did this former-Egyptian-warrior-turned-desert-shepherd have that might have uniquely qualified him for this task?

6. What promise did God make to Moses in verse 12? _____
   Did he keep that promise? (Compare 3:1 with 19:2, 10–11.)

Exodus 15:1–18 (NASB)

¹Then Moses and the sons of Israel sang this song to the LORD, and said,

"I will sing to the LORD, for He is highly exalted;

The horse and its rider He has hurled into the sea.

²The LORD is my strength and song,

And He has become my salvation;

This is my God, and I will praise Him;

My father's God, and I will extol Him.

³The LORD is a warrior;

The LORD is His name.

⁴Pharaoh's chariots and his army He has cast into the sea;

And the choicest of his officers are drowned in the Red Sea.

⁵The deeps cover them;

They went down into the depths like a stone.

⁶Thy right hand, O LORD, is majestic in power,

Thy right hand, O LORD, shatters the enemy.

⁷And in the greatness of Thine excellence Thou dost overthrow those
    who rise up against Thee;

Thou dost send forth Thy burning anger, and it consumes them as chaff.

⁸And at the blast of Thy nostrils the waters were piled up,

The flowing waters stood up like a heap;

The deeps were congealed in the heart of the sea.

⁹The enemy said, 'I will pursue, I will overtake, I will divide the spoil;

My desire shall be gratified against them;

I will draw out my sword, my hand shall destroy them.'

¹⁰Thou didst blow with Thy wind, the sea covered them;

They sank like lead in the mighty waters.

¹¹Who is like Thee among the gods, O LORD?

Who is like Thee, majestic in holiness,

Awesome in praises, working wonders?

¹²Thou didst stretch out Thy right hand,

The earth swallowed them.

¹³In Thy lovingkindness Thou hast led the people whom Thou hast redeemed;

In Thy strength Thou hast guided them to Thy holy habitation.

¹⁴The peoples have heard, they tremble;

Anguish has gripped the inhabitants of Philistia.

¹⁵Then the chiefs of Edom were dismayed;

The leaders of Moab, trembling grips them;

All the inhabitants of Canaan have melted away.

¹⁶Terror and dread fall upon them;

By the greatness of Thine arm they are motionless as stone;

Until Thy people pass over, O LORD,

Until the people pass over whom Thou hast purchased.

¹⁷Thou wilt bring them and plant them in the mountain of Thine inheritance,

The place, O Lord, which Thou hast made for Thy dwelling,

The sanctuary, O Lord, which Thy hands have established.

¹⁸The Lord shall reign forever and ever."

Exodus 15:1–18 Study Questions

A related thought from Patsy:

> Moses got to the Red Sea and had to deal with a bunch of sarcastic people. . . . You know what the people said to Moses? "Hey, Mo, thanks a lot for bringing us out here! Did you guide us out here so we could die?"

1. How do you think you would have reacted when faced with the Red Sea before you and Pharaoh's army behind you? Would you have considered this to be an impossible situation?

   _____
   _____

2. Compare verses 4–10 above with Exodus 14:21–29. List some of the vivid words Moses used to describe the miracle that had just occurred.

   _____
   _____

3. Scan through Moses' song again and list all the words that highlight characteristics of God.

   _____
   _____

4. Has there been a time in your life when God pulled you through what looked like an impossible situation? See if you can rewrite verses 10–12 to describe what God did for you in that situation.

   _____
   _____

A Last Word

An insight from this session to remember until next time

> ## Leader's **NOTES**

Take time to read aloud Patsy's closing remarks before you end this session in prayer. Challenge the women to remember that God is with them, no matter where along their life maps they happen to be today.

Closing Thought: Patsy closes her talk with words of encouragement to us wherever we are on the maps of our lives. Some of us are enjoying restful oases; others are struggling to make it over a steep mountain or through a dry desert.

> Here we are moving through these different places of life until we finally find ourselves at the base of Mount Sinai. The name of the place they camped means "the palm of the hand." And that's where [God] wants to place you. I don't know your heartbreak and your hurt, but I know the One who does. He knows if you're on a mountaintop proclaiming his name; he knows if you're in the darkest pit despairing. He longs to place you in the safety of his hand. Whatever your landscape, the wondrous thing about our God is that he said, "I will be with you. In every place that you go, I will be your Shepherd to lead you through the valley. I will be the One to direct you through your hardships. I will gather you up in my arms when you are grieving, and I will hold you in the palm of my hand." It is a sensational life, but we must plant our feet in truth and walk in the light he gives. And we will begin to see change in the dynamics because of the mercy and the grace of the Lord Jesus Christ.

> SESSION 4

PEACE IN A SENSATIONAL LIFE

THELMA WELLS: Be Anxious for Nothing

Full-Length Option (90 minutes)

Introductions, Welcome, and Opening Prayer (5 minutes)
Setting the Stage (2 minutes to review Thelma's Welcoming Vignette on Tape 1—or to have someone read the vignette script aloud)
Main Event (Tape 2—30 minutes)
Taking It to Heart (15 minutes)
Taking It Home (20 minutes)
Back-Stage Pass—Bible Studies (15 minutes)
A Last Word and Closing Prayer (3 minutes)

Fast-Track Option (60 minutes)

Introductions, Welcome, and Opening Prayer (5 minutes)
Setting the Stage (Read the Welcoming Vignette script on your own before the session begins.)
Main Event (Tape 2—30 minutes)
Taking It to Heart (10 minutes)
Taking It Home (10 minutes)
Back-Stage Pass—Bible Studies (Complete these Bible studies later at your convenience.)
A Last Word and Closing Prayer (5 minutes)

Setting the Stage

> ## Leader's **NOTES**

If you're following the Fast-Track Option, skip now to the Main Event. If you're following the Full-Length Option, during the previous sessions you only used one tape; from this point on you'll be using two. Cue Tape 1 to Thelma's Welcoming Vignette (note that her vignette is fourth in the group, after Marilyn Meberg's), and cue Tape 2 to her main presentation in preparation for the Main Event segment. First play the Welcoming Vignette so the group can enjoy the special style Thelma brings to the subject of sensational living. After you view the Welcoming Vignette, switch to Tape 2 and play Thelma's main presentation.

Thelma's Welcoming Vignette describes her personal struggle with finding peace—in herself and in her family—as she introduces the subject of peace in a sensational life.

Thelma's Welcoming Vignette: Peace Wherever You Are

This weekend you will have the opportunity to meet my two daughters, Vikki and Lesa. Actually, they are my best friends. It hasn't always been that way, though. As a matter of fact, when Vikki was twelve years old she said something to me like, "I'm not you, and I don't want to be like you." Lesa was fourteen years old when she scolded me. She said, "Mama, are you ever going to be home for anything I'm doing?" You see, I was off climbing the corporate ladder, and I thought her daddy was making a really good mama. I really did. However, those two girls really hurt my feelings. I felt bad about it. But I want to tell you what it did do for me: It caused me to open my mind, to listen to my daughters, to understand that I can learn something from them, and that life is full of processes. You see, my daughters had lost their peace because I was not there for them. They also made me lose my peace, because they talked about me real bad! However, we now travel as a ministry team, and that gives me a source of peace. I'm going to talk about peace, but you see, peace isn't just because your daughters travel with you. You can gain peace in the midst of any storm—even when there's grief. You indeed can have peace that surpasses all understanding wherever you are in your life. And I think that's a sensational life!

Main Event

▷ Leader's **NOTES**

Preview the video and complete the questions so you can anticipate your group members' responses. Remember to have the women read through this section quickly before viewing the video presentation to get a sense of Thelma's main points so they're ready to fill in the blanks during the video showing.

Video Presentation by Thelma Wells:
The Peace That Surpasses Allllllllll Understanding

According to Thelma, what does everyone long for? _____

The thing we do that gets in the way of having any peace is this: We _____.

Throughout her presentation, Thelma uses a key passage, Philippians 4:6–7. Her favorite adaptation of this passage goes like this:

> Be anxious for nothing, but in all things by prayer and supplication, with thanksgiving, let your requests be made known to God; and the peace of God, which surpasses all understanding, will guard your hearts and your minds through Christ Jesus.

This passage says that we are to "be anxious for nothing." Thelma points out that there are two words in "nothing": ____ _____.

> *You don't have to pray to pray. . . . You can just say, "Uh-uh, mmmmmm, mmmmm . . . have mercy, Jesus. Lord, help me. . . ." And the Holy Spirit interprets our groans and our moans.*
> —Thelma

We are not to be anxious because we are to ask God's help in "everything" or "_____ things" and, according to Thelma, "There ain't nothing on the other side of 'all.' However, there *is* something on the other side of '_____.'" She likes that, because, says Thelma, "When you see '____' you know something else is coming."

We are to bring *all* things before God by prayer. Thelma defines *prayer* as "the heart's sincere desire _____ or _____."

We are also to bring all things before God by "supplication," which means to pray with _____, without _____, knowing that God has _____ to keep his _____.

> *Supplication is like praying for rain when the sun is shining and getting your umbrella out.*
> —Thelma

The passage says we are to do all of this "with thanksgiving." Thelma knows that "nobody is thankful that they're sick or they're broke or they've gotten a bad report about something or they have broken relationships. That's not what it's talking about, but it's saying be thankful because before the _____ of the _____, God had already _____ _____ _____ . He's just waiting on you to ____ ____ to him."

These verses close with the promise that the peace of God, which surpasses "alllllllll understanding," as Thelma says, _____ your heart (that is, your _____) . . . and it will guard your mind (meaning your intellect) through Christ Jesus. Thelma continued:

I did not realize that I was going to have to use that a whole lot. I mean, a *whole* lot. You see, that was the year when there was a great snow in America. I was scheduled to speak in Philadelphia as well as in Indiana. I called from my home in Dallas to both clients and asked them, because of the weather, if they were still going to do the program. They both said yes.

So I flew out of Dallas in the ice and in the snow into Cincinnati. When I got to Cincinnati, Ohio, the airport closed as soon as we landed. So I went over to the phone, and I called my clients and I said, "I'm in Cincinnati. Are you still going to do the program? If not, I can get a flight right back to Dallas."

The client in Philadelphia said, "No, we are not going to do it. I think the weather is just too bad." The client in Indiana said, "Yeah, come on, we're going to do it."

And so, I had to go try to retrieve my baggage. Because the airport was closed, no flights were going out. I went to the baggage place where I could retrieve my baggage, and I think the man was having a bad day because I asked a simple question, "Give me my bags," and he said, "Your bags are already gone to Philadelphia."

"Impossible . . . because there are no flights going out."

And right then my little attitude got a little off. So I stepped back from the counter, and I started saying, "Be-anxious-for-nothing-but-in-all-things-by-prayer-and-supplication-let-your-petition-be-made-known-and-the-peace-of-God-which-surpasses-all-understanding . . . Be anxious for nothing . . . okay . . . Be anxious for nothing . . . whooooo."

And so I walked back, and I was smiling. I think my attitude was better, too, as I said, "Please, I'm going to the hotel next door. Please send me my bags."

And he said, "Yes ma'am, I'll see what I can do."

Well I just skipped-to-my-Lou on over to the hotel, and in about two hours I had my bags. All was well.

The next morning I got up, and I looked out and there was still ice and snow, so I called my client in Indiana. I said, "Are you still going to do the program?"

They said, "Yes, we're going to do the program. Come on." And so I did. I got on the flight, I went to Indiana, I drove on the ice to my hotel. When I got to the hotel there was a note there for me at the registration desk.

Yeah, you got it.

The note said, "Sorry you came. Class is canceled."

I had to go to my hotel room. "'Be anxious for nothing.' Do you mean *nothing*, God? *Nothing?* I have driven here on ice, I called that woman I don't know how many times, and you mean I'm supposed to be anxious for *nothing*? . . . Okay . . . Lord, help me to not be anxious for this."

So I finally got where I could call the lady.

We had a very cordial conversation. And then at the end of the conversation, she explained this: "And you realize that because we canceled the program, we will not pay you."

I said, "Uhhh, let me call you back." I had to call her back. . . .

"What did you say, God? 'Be anxious for nothing'? I want to hurt her now! She's talking about my money!"

So I finally waited to exhale, and I did. And I called her back . . . after I looked at the contract she had signed. And on the contract (I'm so glad I have contracts!), there was an agreement. I told her, "Our agreement that you signed was that if you cancel a program within seventy-two hours, I will get a portion of my fee. But if you cancel within forty-eight hours, I get *all* my fee." . . . Well I did get it within a month.

God had really preserved me during that time because I didn't go off on those people.

However, in October of that year, I forgot this Scripture. . . .

Thelma kept herself from "going off on" the people who irritated her—first the baggage handler at the airport, then the person in charge of the program that was canceled—by pausing long enough to recite the powerful Scripture verses:

Be _____ for _____, but in all things by _____ and _____, with thanksgiving, let your requests be made known to God; and the _____ of God, which surpasses all_____, will guard your hearts and your minds through Christ Jesus.

A few months later in Thelma's second travel adventure, her flight was delayed, and she arrived in Maryland too late to get to her motel before it closed. At the car-rental counter, she ran into a challenging situation when she forgot the "be anxious for nothing" Scripture. Exasperated, she yelled at the car-rental agent, "Do you know _____ __ ____? My name is Thelma Wells, and I travel globally trying to teach people how ____ ____ _____ _____ when they deal with _____ _____ _____!"

Thelma was finally escorted to her car, and she drove to her motel and found a note that said, "I waited on you until midnight. I left." So she bedded down in her car, a sobering experience, said Thelma, "because in the _____ of the night God finally spoke to me, and I _____ _____."

Thelma said the problem was that she forgot. She asked herself why she hadn't depended on the _____ _____ _____ . She realized she had been operating out of _____ and out of _____. She was operating out of "all those 'ations'" that we have: frustration, aggravation, agitation, humiliation, and not depending on _____ _____ _____ in her to pull up when she needed it most.

The little things in life that are so minute compared with many of the problems that we have are really *nothing*. But some of you are dealing with grief and sickness and hurt and broken relationships, and all those things that just tie us up in knots cause us to lose our _____.

Horatio Gates Spafford was a "Job" of his generation because he lost everything in the _____ _____. His only son died that same year. Spafford and his wife and daughters planned a trip to England. He sent his wife and daughters on before him, and there was a wreck on the sea when two ships collided. He lost his four daughters. Only his _____ was left. She sent a telegram bearing only two words: _____ _____. Upon arriving in England to join his wife, Spafford said to Dwight Moody, "It is _____; the _____ of the Lord be done."

> *When our peace is lost, it's not because God has deserted us; it's because we have forgotten to lean and depend on him.*
> —Thelma

> *My great-grandmother would always say, "Baby, God will make a way." He was with me.*
>
> *—Thelma*

We have a choice. We can choose the _____ that surpasses all understanding, or we can _____ it. God is such an awesome Gentleman. He says to us, "I am near. I am with you in your pain, your sorrow, your agony, your divorce, when you have a bad diagnosis, when you lose someone, when you lose your job. I am with you in every situation. Even as you're growing old, I am with you. Come _____ _____."

Thelma points out that we serve a God who knows everything you're going through. Everything. Before the foundation of the world, before there was a star in space, before there was a moon, before he divided the land from the sea, God already had _____ on his mind. And he gives you a choice. You can accept the _____ that God brings, or you can _____ in the middle of that mess and drown in it.

> *Today is your day of release. God has prepared for you today, this very day, this very hour, healing and deliverance from his Word. Be anxious for nothing! No thing. Nada. Huh-uh.*
>
> *—Thelma*

Taking It to Heart
Questions to help you personalize the lessons in the session

▷ Leader's **NOTES**

Give the group a few moments to work on the following questions. Thelma has shared at length from some personal experiences of remembering Scripture and living by it . . . and forgetting Scripture and trying to go it on her own. Perhaps some of the women in your group will be able to relate.

1. Have you ever had an experience where you did the right thing and followed God's leading even when it was difficult? Describe the situation.

   _____
   _____
   _____
   _____

2. Have you ever had an experience where you did the wrong thing, not following God's leading even though you knew better? What happened? How did you feel about it afterward?

   _____
   _____
   _____
   _____

3. Do you think it's realistic to "be anxious for nothing"? Why or why not?

   _____
   _____
   _____
   _____

4. What types of "-ations" most often cause you to lose your peace?

   _____
   _____
   _____
   _____

5. Why is it that little frustrations can be soooooo irritating?

   _____
   _____
   _____
   _____

Taking It Home
Questions to help you apply the lessons from the session

> ## Leader's **NOTES**
>
> Thelma focused on just a couple of verses of Scripture that talk about peace and then sang a famous hymn about "peace like a river." Take these few minutes to get down to the nitty-gritty of each person's life. The women do not need to share deeply personal issues, but challenge them to be in touch with God in order to find the peace that he promises.

1. What does it mean that we are to "be anxious for nothing"? In your life, what do you need to stop being anxious about?

   _____
   _____
   _____

2. What does it mean to you to know that God is not surprised by anything that happens in your life?

   _____
   _____
   _____

3. Thelma says you have a choice to accept the peace that God brings or to stay in the middle of whatever pain you're in and let it drown you. If you choose to accept God's peace, how are you going to begin to make that decision a practical reality in your life from this moment on?

   _____

4. What do you need to do *today* to be able to say to God, "It is well with my soul"?

Back-Stage Pass—Bible Studies
Scripture passages used by Thelma Wells

> Leader's NOTES

If you're following the Fast-Track Option, direct the group to skip to A Last Word at the end of the session and encourage the women to complete the Bible studies later, at their convenience. If you're following the Full-Length Option, ask one of the women to read each passage aloud, then guide the group through the questions that follow. If time runs out, you may have to complete the Bible studies later at home.

Philippians 4:6–7 (NKJV)

⁶Be anxious for nothing, but in everything by prayer and supplication, with thanksgiving, let your requests be made known to God; ⁷and the peace of God, which surpasses all understanding, will guard your hearts and minds through Christ Jesus.

Philippians 4:6–7 Study Questions

An introductory thought from Thelma:

> Sometimes we need to pull the Scriptures up so that we have the Word of God to give us peace that surpasses understanding.

1. To "pull the Scriptures up" means to have them memorized so that they easily come to mind when you need them. These verses from Philippians may already be in your memory bank (if not, then you need to commit them to memory right now!). In what ways have these verses helped you find peace when you didn't feel peaceful? In what situations could they help you in your everyday routine—or in future situations?

   _____
   _____

2. Thelma did a word study of these verses in her presentation. Do your own exposition. Beside each phrase below, write your own paraphrase.
   Be anxious for nothing _____
   In everything _____
   By prayer _____
   By supplication _____
   With thanksgiving _____
   Let your requests be made known to God _____
   The peace of God, which surpasses all understanding _____
   Guard your heart _____
   Guard your mind _____
   Through Christ Jesus _____

3. Now rewrite the verse so that it applies personally to you. (For example, "I will not be anxious about _____ but I will _____")

   _____
   _____

Isaiah 9:6–7 (NIV)

⁶For to us a child is born,
    to us a son is given,
    and the government will be on his shoulders.
And he will be called
    Wonderful Counselor, Mighty God,
    Everlasting Father, Prince of Peace.
⁷Of the increase of his government and peace
    there will be no end.
He will reign on David's throne
    and over his kingdom,
establishing and upholding it
    with justice and righteousness
    from that time on and forever.
The zeal of the Lord Almighty
    will accomplish this.

Isaiah 9:6–7 Study Questions

1. Thelma notes that Jesus is called the "Prince of Peace." In what ways is this true according to the rest of Scripture? Look up the following verses and write how Jesus is indeed the Prince of Peace.
   Isaiah 53:5 _____
   John 14:27 _____
   Romans 4:25–5:2 _____
   Ephesians 2:12–16 _____
   Colossians 1:16–20 _____

2. Most people would define *peace* as "the absence of conflict." According to John 14:27 (noted in question 1 above), Jesus said he would give peace to his followers. Did he mean

that he would give them "absence of conflict"? Why or why not? (Read Mark 13:5–13 and John 16:33.)

_____
_____

3. If Jesus is not guaranteeing the "absence of conflict," what kind of peace does he give?

_____
_____

3. Galatians 5:22 lists "peace" as a fruit of the Spirit. Do you see the fruit of peace blossoming in your own life? Explain why or why not.

_____
_____

4. According to Isaiah 26:3, what is the way to perfect peace? Explain.

_____
_____

A Last Word
An insight from this session to remember until next time

⟩ Leader's NOTES

Use the words to the hymn "It Is Well with My Soul" as your closing thought. Thelma has sung the words, but now have someone read them aloud. Sometimes hearing them without the music causes them to sink in even more.

SENSATIONAL LIFE

Closing Thought: Thelma has made it clear that in whatever situation we find ourselves, God promises to be with us. Horatio Spafford trusted that this was true even in the midst of devastating loss. His pain caused him to pen these words, which have brought "peace like a river" to many grieving souls. Remember: God is with you, and he says, "Come unto me."

It Is Well with My Soul

When peace, like a river, attendeth my way,
When sorrows like sea-billows roll;
Whatever my lot, Thou hast taught me to say,
It is well, it is well with my soul.

Though Satan should buffet, though trials should come,
Let this blest assurance control,
That Christ hath regarded my helpless estate
And hath shed His own blood for my soul.

My sin—Oh, the bliss of this glorious thought,
My sin—not in part, but the whole,
Is nailed to the cross, and I bear it no more,
Praise the Lord, praise the Lord, O my soul!

And, Lord, haste the day when my faith shall be sight,
The clouds be rolled back as a scroll,
The trump shall resound and the Lord shall descend,
"Even so"—it is well with my soul.

> SESSION 5

ENDURANCE IN A SENSATIONAL LIFE

BARBARA JOHNSON:
Just Another Hurdle in the Road

Full-Length Option (90 minutes)

Introductions, Welcome, and Opening Prayer (5 minutes)

Setting the Stage (There is no Welcoming Vignette by Barbara Johnson. Take just a minute to explain to your group the illness Barbara has been facing by reading the Leader's Notes on page 52.)

Main Event (Tape 2—10 minutes)

Taking It to Heart (15 minutes)

Taking It Home (15 minutes)

Back-Stage Pass—Bible Studies (15 minutes)

A Last Word and Closing Prayer (5 minutes)

Reflection and Discussion Time (Use this extra time wherever it works best for your group—25 minutes)

Fast-Track Option (60 minutes)

Introductions, Welcome, and Opening Prayer (5 minutes)

Setting the Stage (There is no Welcoming Vignette by Barbara Johnson. Take just a minute to explain to your group the illness Barbara has been facing by reading the Leader's Notes on page 52.)

Main Event (Tape 2—10 minutes)

Taking It to Heart (13 minutes)

Taking It Home (12 minutes)

Back-Stage Pass—Bible Studies (15 minutes—at least one passage)

A Last Word and Closing Prayer (5 minutes)

Setting the Stage

▶ Leader's NOTES

Barbara was unable to attend this conference in person—although she appears through a videotaped session that was shown to the attendees. The year before, she had been diagnosed with a malignant brain tumor. She had surgery and chemotherapy, and in her Main Event session, she talks about that experience in an interview with Mary Graham. At the time of this conference, she was still advised by her doctors not to travel. Therefore, while the other speakers' main presentations run thirty or forty minutes long, Barbara's presentation runs only ten minutes.

You will need to consider how you want to use the extra time in your session. If you are doing the Full-Length Option, we suggest that you include an extra twenty-five minutes of reflection and discussion. If you are doing the Fast-Track Option, you should have time to work through at least one passage in the Back-Stage Pass Bible Studies.

One idea is to encourage a longer time of sharing personal stories among the women. Many may already be familiar with Barbara Johnson through her popular books such as *Stick a Geranium in Your Hat and Be Happy* and *Living Somewhere Between Estrogen and Death*. A later book, appropriately titled *Plant a Geranium in Your Cranium*, chronicles her battle with the malignant brain tumor. Barbara and her husband, Bill, are the founders of Spatula Ministries, an outreach to help parents who need to be "scraped off the ceiling" after they've landed there from dealing with a difficult crisis involving their children. Barbara's ministry offers these parents a safe place to find listening ears and sympathetic hearts. "We like to say Spatula peels these parents off the ceiling with a spatula of love and sets them on the road to recovery," says Barbara.

Your group has been together for quite a while now, so the women may feel comfortable enough with each other to share their own fears and concerns either due to their children, their health, or other situations in their lives. You could also use the extra time to pray for one another.

Main Event

> ## Leader's **NOTES**

Preview the video and complete the questions so you can anticipate your group members' responses. The note-taking portion begins right away, and the first quotation comes after Mary's question to Barbara about keeping a sense of humor.

Video Presentation by Barbara Johnson: Either Way, I'm a Winner

The doctor told Barbara the brain tumor and the accompanying surgery and chemotherapy would probably be "the hardest thing" she had ever had to face. Her response was that he surely didn't know what she had had to face in the past. To Barbara, cancer was just another _____ ___ _____ _____.

Barbara said she wasn't afraid because she knew _____ was with her and that he had been with her through all the other problems she had endured. "He's been there. He's been a _____, he's been a _____, he's been a refuge, so I knew he would be with me."

Mary Graham remembered the morning after Barbara's surgery, when the surgeon came into her room. "You had no hair, and staples from ear to ear," Mary said. "And the doctor said to you, 'What is a nickel plus a dime plus a quarter?' I was thinking, *Let's see. A nickel plus a dime . . .* And you said, 'Forty cents.' I thought, *Well, I guess she's okay.*"

Barbara credits her successful recovery from the brain surgery to all the prayers and the _____ that were given to her at that time. After completing chemotherapy, her doctor told her one day, "I don't see any _____ in your brain." Barbara didn't know if that was good or bad! But the doctor meant it as good, that the tumor was resolving and melting.

JUST ANOTHER HURDLE IN THE ROAD   53

> *Cancer is the manure pit of life. But I know God is there in the pit with me, and he can use that ugly mess to fertilize my life with love and hope—and laughter!*
>
> —*Barbara*

Barbara believes God brought her through the cancer experience for a reason: "So maybe I'll have _____ ___ _____ with other people who are going through similar situations."

Barbara has often been called the "queen of encouragement." During her ordeal with cancer, other people encouraged *her* through cards, letters, phone, calls, and prayers. Some of her friends even gave her a _____ shower.

Question: Barbara, how did you manage to keep your sense of humor?

Answer: Well, I think I was born with one, and if you don't have one you have to borrow one, beg one, or steal one because a sense of humor is the only thing that's gotten me through the devastating things that have happened in my life. You know, I picked my husband up off the highway after a car accident, then I lost a son a couple of years after that in Vietnam, then in five years I lost another son who was killed by a drunk driver. And then our darling third son, who was the joy of our home, disappeared and we had an eleven-year estrangement from him. (We did have a restoration after that.)

So I've already had four big whoppers in my life, and I managed to keep a sense of humor though all those things. God has brought me through these things; I'm not taking any credit that I'm so strong, but he's given strength, and because of the strength he's imparted to me, we've come through those four different things, and this is just one more hurdle.

I have two boys who both have a good sense of humor—I have two boys here and two boys in heaven. But the two boys who are here both have a real good sense of humor, and they're just lots of fun.

One morning in the hospital I woke up at about 4:30, . . . and I heard the music for the *Little House on the Prairie.* I thought, *Oh, I love that program. That's my favorite program. I wonder who is playing that at this time of the morning?*

Somebody was holding my hand—and it was my son Barney. Big, tall, six-foot-two, 210 pounds, watching *Little House on the Prairie* and holding my hand. That was real meaningful to me, that he came at that time of the day. God is showing me so many qualities in my boys that I didn't know before I had this happen. It brought them closer together, and to each other, and to me. I'm thankful for this experience. Anything that brings you closer to the Lord and to your family, it's got to be a good thing.

If I could say anything to the people who are out there who are maybe facing cancer: First, I'd tell them to read my book *Plant a Geranium in Your Cranium!* I think that book, because it was written during the dark time of my life—the time after surgery—has enough wisdom and enough insight spiritually to encourage anybody, whether you're facing cancer or just facing the dark places in life. So I felt a real assurance as I did that book that it is going to be a real lifesaver for many people. . . .

Spiritually, I've had more blessings than most anybody. I have two boys in heaven—deposits in heaven—and I have two here on earth. So when I wake up, if I wake up in heaven, I'm with my two sons who are in heaven, and if I'm still here, then I'm with my two that I have here. So I can't lose either way, right? I can't lose. I'm a winner either way.

Before she was diagnosed with a malignant brain tumor, Barbara had already endured four "whoppers" in her life:
1. Her husband's ____ _____.
2. One son who was killed in _____.
3. Another son who was killed by ____ _____ _____.
4. The estrangement of a third son for _____ years.

Barbara says a sense of _____ played a big part in her survival.

An unexpected blessing in Barbara's family that came out of her time of illness and hospitalization was that God showed her many qualities in her sons that she didn't know they had. Her illness brought her sons closer to each other, and to her. Thus, Barbara says, "I'm _____ for

> *I think I was born with a sense of humor. If you don't have one, you have to borrow one, beg one, or steal one.*
> —Barbara

this experience. If something brings you closer to the _____ or to your _____, it's got to be a good thing."

Barbara says she's a winner no matter what happens in her future. "I have two boys in _____ . . . and I have two here on_____. So when I wake up, if I wake up in heaven, I'm with my two sons who are in heaven, and if I'm still here, then I'm with my two that I have here. So I _____ _____ either way. . . . I'm a winner either way.

> *It's the prayers of God's people that have brought healing to my heart and to my body.*
>
> *—Barbara*

Taking It to Heart
Questions to help you personalize the lessons in the session

> **Leader's NOTES**
>
> Give the group a few moments to work on these questions alone before you invite sharing.

1. Barbara has been through a lot of "whoppers" in her life. In what ways has God used those experiences in her life and ministry?

   _____
   _____
   _____

2. How is it possible to have a sense of humor in difficult situations?

   _____
   _____

3. How does the ability to laugh help to keep life bearable?

   _____
   _____

4. Describe Barbara's perspective on her life and on her future. How does her perspective help her keep going?

_____
_____
_____

5. Barbara talks a lot about the prayers and encouragement from God's people that have helped her so much. How does this help you when it comes to knowing what to do when a friend is dealing with a difficult situation?

_____
_____
_____

Taking It Home
Questions to help you apply the lessons from the session

> ## Leader's **NOTES**
>
> You probably have some women in your group who have firsthand knowledge of cancer and chemotherapy. If not, someone in your group will know someone who has gone through this. Because you have extra time in this session, allow people to share their feelings about these situations.

1. If you have dealt with cancer, what types of encouragement were most helpful to you? How would you advise others to help those who are facing cancer and chemotherapy?

_____
_____

2. What was *not* helpful? In other words, what would you advise people *not* to do?

3. How is having an eternal perspective most helpful during difficult times?

4. In her book *Plant a Geranium in Your Cranium,* Barbara writes, "A sense of humor is a key component of a life filled with joy and optimism. . . . For many of us, it *does* take work to find joy in the world around us. We have to keep *choosing* to look for it in unexpected places." How can you begin to take Barbara's advice and look for joy in unexpected places?

Back-Stage Pass—Bible Studies
Scripture passages used by Barbara Johnson

> Leader's NOTES

Even if you're following the Fast-Track Option, you probably will have time to do at least one of the studies that follow because Barbara's message is so brief. If you're following the Full-Length Option, ask one of the women to read each passage aloud, then guide the group through the questions. Barbara does not refer to any particular Bible passages in her interview. She briefly mentions what God meant to her during her darkest days. Her words are taken from Psalm 18, which is studied here. The second Bible passage is quoted on page 82 of her latest book, *Plant a Geranium in Your Cranium,* and so has been chosen to study here.

58   SENSATIONAL LIFE

Psalm 18:2–6 (NIV)

²The LORD is my rock, my fortress and my deliverer;
   my God is my rock, in whom I take refuge.
   He is my shield and the horn of my salvation, my stronghold.
³I call to the LORD, who is worthy of praise,
   and I am saved from my enemies.
⁴The cords of death entangled me;
   the torrents of destruction overwhelmed me.
⁵The cords of the grave coiled around me;
   the snares of death confronted me.
⁶In my distress I called to the LORD;
   I cried to my God for help.
From his temple he heard my voice;
   my cry came before him, into his ears.

Psalm 18:2–6 Study Questions

1. Barbara noted that, through the dark days of chemotherapy, God was her rock, her fortress, and her deliverer. David, the psalmist, wrote those words. Why do you think those are appropriate images for God, especially when we are faced with health or family challenges? Fill in the blanks below.

   In times of suffering, God is a rock because
   _____
   _____.

   In times of suffering, God is a fortress because
   _____
   _____.

   In times of suffering, God is a deliverer because
   _____
   _____.

2. Have you ever felt as David did—that "cords of death entangled" you, that "torrents of destruction overwhelmed" you? If so, describe the situation.

___

3. What does it mean to you that you can cry to God for help and he will hear you—that your cry goes right to his ears?

___

4. Is it easy or difficult for you to call on God? Why?

___

2 Corinthians 4:8–9, 16–17 (TLB)

⁸We are pressed on every side by troubles, but not crushed and broken. We are perplexed because we don't know why things happen as they do, but we don't give up and quit. ⁹We are hunted down, but God never abandons us. We get knocked down, but we get up again and keep going. . . . ¹⁶That is why we never give up. Though our bodies are dying, our inner strength in the Lord is growing every day. ¹⁷These troubles and sufferings of ours are, after all, quite small and won't last very long. Yet this short time of distress will result in God's richest blessing upon us forever and ever!

2 Corinthians 4:8–9, 16–17 Study Questions

1. List below the four contrasts made in verses 8 and 9. In the first blank, write what Paul says happens to us. After the "but," write how we react (or should react).

   We are _____, but _____.
   We are _____, but _____.
   We are _____, but _____.
   We are _____, but _____.

2. According to Paul, why do we never give up?
   _____
   _____

3. No time of distress seems "short" when we are in it. How, then, can Paul call this a "short time of distress"?
   _____
   _____
   _____

4. What will be the result of this time of distress?
   _____
   _____

5. Read James 1:2–4. In what ways can you be joyful even in times of trouble?
   _____
   _____
   _____

A Last Word
An insight from this session to remember until next time

> ## Leader's **NOTES**
>
> Take time to read the closing quotation from Barbara's book (reprinted below) before you end the session with prayer. Encourage your group members to start to look for joy in unexpected places, to learn to laugh again, even when the going is tough. They cannot change their situations, but they can change their attitudes toward their situations—and that makes all the difference in having a sensational life!

Closing Thought: The following quotation is taken from Barbara's book *Plant a Geranium in Your Cranium*. It seems to be a fitting closing to this lesson.

> I don't want you to think I'm saying that having cancer is a breeze—just smile and be happy and everything will be fine. In fact, it is awful. So don't think there was any courage on my part; I was just facing what was put before me. . . .
>
> Of course, any job's always easier when it's done joyfully—and gratefully. Sometimes—when we're diagnosed with a serious illness, for example—we don't feel like being grateful. Or we may feel ashamed that we are so needy, ashamed to acknowledge the help we have already received and the help we will need in the future. Oh, but if we can get past that shameful obstacle and for *all* things give thanks, what a difference it makes in our lives.
>
> God doesn't really need our gratitude, but *we* need to be grateful! A thankful heart deepens our faith and enhances the quality of our lives. That's why we need to turn to God on sunny days as well as those times when storms wreck our lives. Counting our blessings is a sure way to enrich our daily journey. Tally up your simple blessings and simple treasures every chance you get. Write them down and marvel at how long the list grows. Develop the habit of thankfulness, and it will lead to a life of optimistic thinking.

> SESSION 6

WHOLENESS IN A SENSATIONAL LIFE

MARILYN MEBERG: Gun It!

Full-Length Option (90 minutes)

Introductions, Welcome, and Opening Prayer (3 minutes)

Setting the Stage (2 minutes to review Marilyn's Welcoming Vignette on Tape 1—or to have someone read the vignette script aloud)

Main Event (Tape 2—40 minutes)

Taking It to Heart (13 minutes)

Taking It Home (15 minutes)

Back-Stage Pass—Bible Studies (15 minutes)

A Last Word and Closing Prayer (2 minutes)

Fast-Track Option (60 minutes)

Introductions, Welcome, and Opening Prayer (4 minutes)

Setting the Stage (Read the Welcoming Vignette script on your own before the session begins.)

Main Event (Tape 2—40 minutes)

Taking It to Heart (7 minutes)

Taking It Home (7 minutes)

Back-Stage Pass—Bible Studies (Complete these Bible studies later at your convenience.)

A Last Word and Closing Prayer (2 minutes)

Setting the Stage

> ## Leader's NOTES

If you're following the Fast-Track Option, skip now to the Main Event. If you're following the Full-Length Option, have Tape 1 cued to Marilyn's Welcoming Vignette.

Play the vignette during the Setting the Stage segment. Have Tape 2 cued so it's ready to play Marilyn's main presentation.

Marilyn's Welcoming Vignette talks about how misconceptions can confuse us. Sensational experiences do not necessarily make a sensational life.

Marilyn's Welcoming Vignette: Milky Misconceptions

Margaret was a missionary who lay dying in bed with the complications of pneumonia. The other twelve women, who served with her on a little self-perpetuating farm where they would translate Scripture and then tell it to the people who would come and listen and be instructed by them, were just devastated at the possible loss of Margaret. She had been such a leader to them.

Elizabeth, particularly, was concerned. She went into the kitchen, thinking, *Surely I can get some liquid down her throat. She must be so parched.* She found a bottle of brandy that had been given to the compound at Christmas. She knew nothing of its contents, but the bottle was pretty. So she poured a little into the glass and then topped the glass with milk. She took it in to Margaret, lifted her head, and offered her a sip. And then another sip, and then another sip, until ultimately the glass was drained.

Laying Margaret back down on the pillow, the women were so thrilled to see some participation in life that they leaned into the bed and said, "Margaret, do you have anything to say to us?"

"*Never* sell that cow!"

Margaret was obviously suffering a few misconceptions. And I think sometimes we do, too. We need to make the distinction between sensational life and sensational experience. We're going to talk about that difference.

Main Event

> ## Leader's NOTES
>
> When you preview the video, use the PAUSE button on your video machine to give yourself time to fill in some of the answers below. That way you'll be able, after the presentation, to help those who might have missed some things along the way. Encourage the group to scan the questions before watching the tape but not to be overly concerned about taking notes. They don't want to miss a minute of Marilyn's adventures!

Marilyn tells some memorable stories as she illustrates three "arenas" in which God offers us opportunities for sensational living: sensational stretching, sensational second chances, and sensational security. A transcript is provided later in this segment for her final story. It appears under the subhead "Sensational Security: Life Instead of Ashes." As Marilyn illustrates the first two arenas, you can fill in the blanks, and then read along with her as she uses the poignant story of the girl with the paint can to close her presentation.

Video Presentation by Marilyn Meberg: Gun It!

Marilyn had a "sensational" time on that "hill-hopper" excursion, but she makes the point that we need to make a distinction between a sensational _____ and a sensational _____.

A sensational experience has a _____, a _____, and an _____.

The hill-hopper excursion qualified as only a sensational experience because it eventually ended, and the next day Marilyn found herself back in another _____ _____.

According to Marilyn, sensational experiences don't last. But, she says, "It is possible to not live within the reality of just sensational experience but to have sensational life every single day that does not have a beginning, a middle, and an end, and it's predicated on _____. It is knowing him."

> *God is sensational, and everything you and I experience is sensational when we're held by him.*
>
> —Marilyn

Marilyn makes the point that some people might ask, "Marilyn, do you read the papers? Do you look into your own life and the lives of those around you? Life is _____ _____!"

She answers that sensational living has to do with being "absolutely surrounded, encompassed, and held in the protective love of the God of the universe that I know personally through Jesus as Savior, [which] makes every experience sensational, even though there's _____ in it."

Watching her beloved husband, Ken, die of pancreatic cancer was the hardest thing she's ever experienced, said Marilyn. "But here's what is so peculiar to the believer who is held in the security of the God of the universe and his protective, sensational security. . . . In that worst of experiences I felt his _____, I knew his _____, and I knew his _____."

We can have sensational living in spite of painful times, Marilyn says, "because _____ is sensational, and everything you and I experience is sensational when we're held by him."

Marilyn suggests there are three arenas in which God makes it clear to us that there are sensational living opportunities: sensational stretching, sensational second chances, and sensational security.

Sensational Stretching: Living Beyond the Comfort Zone

Marilyn illustrates sensational stretching in a story about Paul Cho, pastor of the largest church in the world, in Korea. As Paul Cho's ministry began to spread and became increasingly broad and then international, he made a deal with God. He said he would "go anywhere you want me to go. I will preach to anyone what it is to know Jesus as Savior, . . . but I cannot be asked to give that message to the _____. I'll go anywhere else."

She explained that "the cultural differences, pain, and atrocities each nation had perpetrated on the other during various wars had left tremendous pain, deep hurt, enormous resentment, hatred, and prejudice in the heart of Paul Cho. And the thought of sharing Jesus with the Japanese was more than he could handle."

So what did God do? He sent Paul Cho to be the keynote speaker at a huge rally and conference for pastors in _____. When he was introduced, Paul "walked to the podium, looked out over that sea of Japanese faces, and was overwhelmed with one emotion, and he stated it: 'I _____ you.'" The pastors responded by walking up to the podium one by one, kneeling down at Paul Cho's feet, and asking, "Will you _____ _____?"

At the end of this dramatic exchange, "Paul melted. . . . He looked out again at these people, and he smiled and said, 'I _____ _____.'"

Marilyn explained, "When we're stretched it's that we might experience more deeply, more fully the _____ of God . . . the sensational, encompassing _____ of God. Paul did as he was stretched to the point way beyond his _____ _____ _____. God brought that about. That's the characteristic element of being stretched."

She also shares a touching story about Women of Faith's prayer intercessor, Lana Bateman, who cared for her mother-in-law as the woman, who had despised Lana for years and was not a believer, died of cancer. A few days before her mother-in-law died, Lana asked her simply, "What about _____?"

Her mother-in-law replied, "He must be here—because _____ _____."

> *Did it ever occur to you that when you and I blow it, God doesn't say, "Well! I can't use them now"?*
>
> —Marilyn

Eventually the mother-in-law "asked Jesus, the one whom she had scoffed at and reviled—asked Jesus to come into her heart and to forgive her for her bitterness and her prejudice. And she died, and she went to heaven, where she is now," said Marilyn.

If you find yourself caring for people you don't like and who haven't liked you, you may think, *I can't do it.* Marilyn answers, "No, you can't. _____ does it, and you join forces with him and you remember that as you are being stretched you are also growing. Sensational stretching is sensational _____ in a new way with the God of the universe."

Sensational Second Chances: God Can Still Use You

Jonah was an Old Testament prophet. God told him to go to Ninevah and tell the people if they didn't stop doing what they were doing and repent of their sins, he would wipe them out. But Jonah thought it would be great idea to wipe them out because the Ninevites were people who despised the _____ and, "in their pagan behavior, loved nothing more than to cut the heads off of these Jewish people, line them up and make various designs outside the villages before they burned them down," said Marilyn. No wonder Jonah didn't want to go to Ninevah and boarded a ship going somewhere else!

But he got a second chance after he was swallowed by a big fish—which later vomited him up close to shore. God said to Jonah, "_____ and go to Ninevah." He didn't say, "You're no _____." He didn't say, "When I give you a call and you disobey it, I'll never be able to use you. You have absolutely outlasted your usefulness—I saved your life, but I can't _____ your life." Instead God said, "____ to _____."

Marilyn points out that the wicked, pagan people of Ninevah also got a second chance. She explains, "God is not affected by our _____. He's affected by our ability and our

_____ to him. When God calls us to himself, no matter what our culture, no matter what our background, no matter how many times we've been disobedient, he reaches out for us and _____ _____ to him. That's what _____ is, and that's what grace is, and that's what Jesus provided on the cross.

Scripture says the Ninevites heard Jonah's message and "every single person in Ninevah repented, turned around, and came to know and love Jehovah God."

The apostle Peter also needed a second chance. "This impetuous, undisciplined, perhaps even unbalanced apostle said to Jesus shortly before the crucifixion, 'I'm not going to _____ you. I'm sticking by you.'" But when Jesus was arrested and hauled away for crucifixion, Peter cowered. In his cowardice, he denied Jesus three times: "I _____ _____ never knew him. No, no, you've got the wrong person. I've never been with him."

After the resurrection, Jesus, in an effort to reconnect with his disciples, and very specifically, to shore up the hurt and the pain of Peter, had a little fish fry on the shores of the Sea of Galilee. He took Peter aside and asked, "Peter, do you _____ me?"

Peter said, "Yes."
Jesus said, "Peter, do you love me?"
"Yes, Lord, I love you."
"Peter, do you love me?"
"Yes, Lord."

Marilyn notes, "How gracious of God, in the second chance he gave Peter. He gave Peter _____ opportunities to wipe out three _____." She points out that earlier, Jesus had said to Peter, "Upon you I will build my church."

Sensational Security: Life Instead of Ashes

Marilyn illustrates sensational security with a true story from Ravi Zacharias's book *Cries of the Heart:*

Ravi had received a newsletter from a place called Covenant House in New York City. It's run by the Catholic Church. They dealt with kids and offered homes and clothing and warm food and a warm environment for those who had no place to go. These sisters would provide for the children's needs when they came to the house.

One cold November night, there's a knock at the door, and one of the sisters goes to the door, and standing there on the doorstep is a little girl, about fourteen, wet with the rain, shivering with the cold, and of course the sister invited her to come in. Now, this was not an unusual sight for the Catholic sister to see, because this was their ministry. But it was unusual to see that this little girl had clutched in both arms a paint can. And as this little girl was showering, eating, sleeping, the paint can was always near her. In the shower, it was outside the shower; in the bed, it was right next to her bed; when she ate it was between her ankles. Days went by, and the sisters watched with a certain amount of curiosity and even confusion at this little girl—Kathy was her name. What could the paint can be about?

One day they noted that she was in a kind of side room in Covenant House. She was holding the painting can, the hair falling forward, crying and talking softly and singing and rocking the paint can. One of the sisters, overwhelmed with curiosity and compassion, came over and said, "Kathy, I don't want to intrude, but would you please tell me, What is in your paint can?"

Kathy said, "It's my mother."

She said, "When I was two days old I was thrown into a dumpster in New York City. The police heard me, and I was raised in one foster home after another, tremendously angry and resentful, wondering how could anyone do that. I became acquainted with some people who promised to help me find this woman because I wanted to tell her I hated her and ask her how could she possibly have thrown me into a dumpster. We finally found my mother at a local hospital in New York City. When I went into her room I was told by the nurse that she was dying of AIDS."

She said, "Something inside me changed when I looked at her. She was so skinny and frail. She looked awful. And I couldn't go over to that skinny, awful-looking woman and tell her I hated her. But I did go over to her and tell her who I was, that I was the baby she had thrown into a dumpster. And you know what, Sister?" said Kathy. "She apologized. She said, 'I'm so sorry, honey. I'm so sorry.' And that helped me. The next day I was going to back and see her again and bring her something, but she died in the night. Those people at the hospital were so nice to me. They gave me her cremains, and they're in this bucket. And look: You can see the date of her birth and the date of her death and her name. Don't take her away."

The sister said, "Of course not. We'll never take it away."

The security that this little Kathy needed then, that you and I need now—Scripture addresses that need for security. In Psalm 27:10 we read, "Though my mother and my father abandon me, you will hold me close." Isaiah 41:9: "I have chosen you. I'll never throw you away."

We've all been thrown away by circumstances or people. We've all longed to be held with the security of someone we felt loved us. And the God of the universe loves us to such an incredible degree that he offers us life instead of ashes. Jesus said, "I am the way and the truth and the life."

Little Kathy was holding ashes. Sometimes you and I are holding ashes in the hope of a relationship yet to materialize—in the hope of a job that proves to be less than we thought, other relationships, a home, a car. You name it. What we hope for, unless it's made up of God and his presence, is ashes. It has no life. Only Jesus has life.

(Marilyn's invitation and closing prayer are reprinted in A Last Word, page 78.)

Taking It to Heart
Questions to help you personalize the lessons in the session

⊙ Leader's **NOTES**

This lesson has been a bit longer than some of the others, so if you find yourself running low on time, you might want to launch into a brief discussion of these questions without giving extra time for the group members to work on them on their own. Be aware that someone in your group may have responded to Marilyn's invitation to receive Christ. Her closing prayer and the suggestions in A Last Word will help you acknowledge and celebrate that decision.

1. Describe an experience in your life when, looking back, you realize God was stretching you into a new, closer relationship with him.

2. Have you ever been given a "second chance" by God? Describe the situation.

3. How does it make you feel to know that God never says, "I'll never be able to use you. You have absolutely outlasted your usefulness—I *saved* your life, but I can't *use* your life"?

4. How does knowing this about God contribute to your ability to look at your life as "sensational"?

Taking It Home
Questions to help you apply the lessons from the session

▷ Leader's NOTES

The responses to the questions in the Taking It to Heart section may have given you a better sense of where your group is spiritually. Some may have shared some "stretching experiences" or "second chances" they are facing right now. The lines below are meant for each woman to journal her thoughts on what God might be saying to her right now about how he is stretching her, offering her a second chance, or providing sensational security. If you don't have time to discuss these issues today, ask your group members to take the time in the coming week to listen to God regarding these questions.

Perhaps Marilyn has hit a chord with you today. Consider the situations in your life right now. Maybe you feel you are being stretched to deal with a new situation in life—a situation you would rather run from than face. What should you do differently?

_____
_____
_____

Maybe you are being given a second chance in an area where you have failed in the past. What is God saying to you today about getting back up and letting him use you?

_____
_____
_____

Marilyn said, "What we hope for, unless it's made up of God and his presence, is ashes. It has no life. Only Jesus has life." When in your life—in the past or the present—have you clung to ashes instead of the security Jesus offers through a personal relationship with him? How would you respond differently now?

_____
_____
_____

If you have never received Jesus as your Savior, what questions do you still have that are keeping you from taking that important step?

_____
_____
_____

Back-Stage Pass—Bible Studies
Scripture passages used by Marilyn Meberg

▸ Leader's **NOTES**

If you're following the Fast-Track Option, direct the women to skip to A Last Word at the end of the session and complete the Bible studies later, at their convenience. If your group is following the Full-Length Option, ask one of the women to read each passage aloud, then guide the women through the questions that follow. The first passage, the story of Jonah, may be very familiar, but it is worth a second look at his second chance. The other passage describes the apostle Peter's second chance.

Jonah 2:1–9

¹While Jonah was inside the fish,
he prayed to the LORD his God and said,
²"When I was in danger,
 I called to the LORD,
 and he answered me.
I was about to die,
 so I cried to you,
 and you heard my voice.
³You threw me into the sea,
 down, down into the deep sea.
The water was all around me,
 and your powerful waves flowed over me.
⁴I said, 'I was driven out of your presence,

    but I hope to see your Holy Temple again.'
⁵The waters of the sea closed around my throat.
    The deep sea was all around me;
    seaweed was wrapped around my head.
⁶When I went down to where the mountains of the sea start to rise,
    I thought I was locked in this prison forever,
but you saved me from the pit of death,
    L ORD my God.
⁷When my life had almost gone,
    I remembered the L ORD.
I prayed to you,
    and you heard my prayers in your Holy Temple.
⁸People who worship useless idols
    give up their loyalty to you.
⁹But I will praise and thank you
    while I give sacrifices to you,
    and I will keep my promises to you.
Salvation comes from the L ORD!"

Jonah 2:2–9 Study Questions

1. Jonah had run away from God when God had given him a second chance. What could God have allowed to happen to Jonah in the course of his attempt to run away?

2. The Bible says, "The L ORD caused a big fish to swallow Jonah" (Jonah 1:17). What does that tell you about God's plans for *your* life? In other words, are you able to run from them or ruin them?

3. In the fish, Jonah prayed fervently to God (wouldn't you?). What do you find interesting in his prayer for help?

   _____
   _____

4. When Jonah was told a second time to go to Nineveh, he went (see 3:1–3). Do you think it was any easier for him that time? Why or why not?

   _____
   _____

5. God was gracious to Jonah. He was also gracious to the Ninevites (see 3:5–10, 4:11). Why did God show grace?

   _____
   _____

6. When you realize that you are being given a second chance, what should you do?

   _____
   _____

Matthew 26:35

But Peter said, "I will never say that I don't know you! I will even die with you!"

Matthew 26:69–74

[69]At that time, as Peter was sitting in the courtyard, a servant girl came to him and said, "You also were with Jesus of Galilee."

[70]But Peter said to all the people there that he was never with Jesus. He said, "I don't know what you are talking about."

[71]When he left the courtyard and was at the gate, another girl saw him. She said to the people there, "This man was with Jesus of Nazareth."

[72]Again, Peter said he was never with him, saying, "I swear I don't know this man Jesus!"

⁷³A short time later, some people standing there went to Peter and said, "Surely you are one of those who followed Jesus. The way you talk shows it."

⁷⁴Then Peter began to place a curse on himself and swear, "I don't know the man." At once a rooster crowed.

John 21:15-17

¹⁵When they finished eating, Jesus said to Simon Peter, "Simon son of John do you love me more than these?"

He answered, "Yes, Lord, you know that I love you."

Jesus said, "Feed my lambs."

¹⁶Again Jesus said, "Simon son of John do you love me?"

He answered, "Yes, Lord, you know that I love you."

Jesus said, "Take care of my sheep."

¹⁷A third time he said, "Simon son of John do you love me?"

Peter was hurt because Jesus asked him the third time, "Do you love me?" Peter said, "Lord, you know everything; you know that I love you!"

He said to him, "Feed my sheep."

Matthew 26:35, 26:69-74; John 21:15-17 Study Questions

1. How do you think Peter felt that day on the beach as Jesus questioned him about his love?

_____
_____

2. Jesus could have told Peter, "I can't use you now." But he didn't. Peter could have felt so remorseful over his denials that, like Judas, he wanted to kill himself. But he didn't. Instead, Peter became the "Rock" that fulfilled the purpose Jesus had for him. What was that purpose? Read Matthew 16:18-19.

_____
_____

3. What did Peter go on to do only weeks later? Read Acts 2:14–15, 36–41.

   _____

   _____

4. Peter wrote a letter to believers who were suffering persecution for their faith. Read 1 Peter 5:6–11. How do you think his experience recorded in the Gospels of Matthew and John quoted above influenced the words he wrote here?

   _____

   _____

A Last Word

An insight from this session to remember until next time

> Leader's NOTES

Marilyn presented the gospel message. If someone has become a new believer in the course of this lesson, set aside a few minutes to celebrate and to pray as a group for her. Anyone who does respond to Christ for the first time is invited to inform Women of Faith of her decision so that a New Testament can be sent to her. A response-card format is included at the end of this lesson.

Closing Thought: As Peter said to the crowds at Pentecost, "Repent and be baptized, every one of you, in the name of Jesus Christ for the forgiveness of your sins. And you will receive the gift of the Holy Spirit. The promise is for you and your children and for all who are far off—for all whom the Lord our God will call" (Acts 2:38–39 NIV). And as Paul wrote, "Today is the day of salvation" (2 Corinthians 6:2 NLT). If you have not placed your trust in Christ, you may have written some questions and concerns under the Taking It

Home section above. Don't leave those questions unanswered. Talk to your group leader or someone you trust. You can begin experiencing the sensational life *today!* Remember Marilyn's words:

How do you get to know that life? It's in a relationship. When this verse in Isaiah says, "I have chosen you," what does that mean? It means, "I've chosen you to be mine. I've chosen you to be in the family of God. I've chosen you to know me through Jesus." There's an interesting metaphor that is used in Revelation 3:20: "Behold, I stand at the door and knock. If anyone hears my voice, I'll come in." God, in the form of Jesus and the Holy Spirit, knocks at the heart-door of our consciousness and says, "Will you let me in? Will you let me in, that I might fill your bucket with life—that I might give you sensational life?"

Right now, at this minute, there may be some of you who are thinking, *I like that!* There may be some of you, if you're very, very quiet, may even experience that knock at your heart-door. I'd like to give you this chance right now to pray and ask Jesus to come on through the door and enter your heart and your life and fill your bucket with life and promise and sensational living.

If you like, with your eyes closed, you could pray possibly these words:

Jesus, there's a lot I don't understand, but I know I've been thrown away, and I would love to have the God of the universe wrap me up in his arms. I would love to know that my sin is forgiven, and when you say you forgive sin, I ask you to do that right now, this minute. Whew! I've done a lot! I don't deserve all these chances, but Lord Jesus, come in through the door. Forgive my sin. Fill me with yourself, which is life everlasting. Thank you, thank you. Amen.

If indeed you did do that, so simply Jesus comes on through the door at your invitation, and you leave here with sensational living because of him.

And then Marilyn adds "one little human touch as you begin your sensational living." She says: *"Gun it!"*

At this point in the conference Women of Faith president Mary Graham asks the women in the auditorium to remain quietly in their seats in consideration of those who are making this life-changing decision. She asks them to fill out a response card similar to the form provided here. At the bottom of the form is a little box. If you have decided to open the door of your heart, put your faith in Christ, and have a personal relationship with God, *check the box.*

To celebrate this sensational decision with you, Women of Faith wants to send you a free copy of the New Testament.

We want to hear from you! Please photocopy the form that follows, provide the information requested, then *check the box* (meaning you have just accepted Christ), and mail the form to us at

DECISION

Women of Faith

820 West Spring Creek Parkway, Suite 400

Plano, TX 75023

Date: _____

Name: _____

Address: _____

_____

E-mail address: _____

Tell us how you're using the *Sensational Life: An Interactive Guide*:

_____ On my own

_____ In a group associated with (the name and address of the church or other organization that's sponsoring your sessions) _____

_____

❑

> SESSION 7

CELEBRATION IN A SENSATIONAL LIFE

LUCI SWINDOLL: The Real Reason to Celebrate

Full-Length Option (90 minutes)

Introductions, Welcome, and Opening Prayer (5 minutes)
Setting the Stage (2 minutes to review Luci's Welcoming Vignette on Tape 1—or to have someone read the vignette script aloud)
Main Event (Tape 3—35 minutes)
Taking It to Heart (15 minutes)
Taking It Home (15 minutes)
Back-Stage Pass—Bible Studies (15 minutes)
A Last Word and Closing Prayer (3 minutes)

Fast-Track Option (60 minutes)

Introductions, Welcome, and Opening Prayer (3 minutes)
Setting the Stage (Read the Welcoming Vignette script on your own before the session begins.)
Main Event (Tape 3—35 minutes)
Taking It to Heart (10 minutes)
Taking It Home (10 minutes)
Back-Stage Pass—Bible Studies (Complete these Bible studies later at your convenience.)
A Last Word and Closing Prayer (2 minutes)

Setting the Stage

Leader's NOTES

If you're following the Fast-Track Option, skip now to the Main Event. If you're following the Full-Length Option, have Tape 1 cued to Luci's Welcoming Vignette. Play the vignette during the Setting the Stage segment. Then cue Tape 3 to be ready to play Luci's main presentation.

Luci's Welcoming Vignette gives a keen insight into how Luci views life. She loves to see every moment as a celebration!

Luci's Welcoming Vignette: Chili-Can Life Mottoes

I'm going to be talking about celebrating, and that is one of the things I love to do the most in life—have a good time, celebrate. In fact, I thought I'd like to have a little motto that I could just carry in my heart forever. Most people get their mottoes from God's Word, but I got mine from a chili can. The other day I was opening a can of chili to have lunch while watching *Law and Order* (my favorite program). I sat down to have lunch—chili—and I looked on the back, and there was the motto written right there about the chili: "Known to cause spontaneous celebrations!" I wore that can of chili around my neck for six days! I hope that your motto can be, "I am celebrating in my relationship with Jesus Christ!" I hope that your life will be one of celebration because of the sensational life God has given you in Christ.

Main Event

> ## Leader's NOTES
>
> Ask group members to take a moment to review the fill-in-the-blanks below so that they will be cued in to what to listen for as they follow along and jot notes.

Luci has learned that God still wants to teach her new things. God has ways of moving her out of her comfort zone and teaching her to trust in him.

Video Presentation by Luci Swindoll: Holding Nothing Back

My best friend when I was a little girl was named Hazel Rhodes. Hazel was just delightful, but my favorite thing about Hazel was her daddy—he owned a candy store. "Owen Rhodes the candy man" is what we used to call him. And from time to time, he would give my dad candy bars—he and my dad were good friends—to give to us kids, me and my two brothers. . . . Daddy would come home with Mars bars and Hershey bars and all kinds of wonderful chocolate candy, and I loved that. But my favorite thing was bubblegum. I just loved blowing great big bubbles and having them plop all over my face. You remember the kind with the funnies in it and they rolled up on the end? Bazooka!

One time Daddy came home and he had three *boxes* of Bazooka bubblegum—one hundred pieces in each box! I had died and gone to heaven! I was thrilled to death! . . . We had Bazooka bubblegum coming out the wazoo! And we were trading back and forth, and we would use it for payment and barter and exchanges. We would . . . have bubble-blowing contests. We had so much. We shared it with everybody, gave it to the neighbors, gave it to Mother and Daddy (and they gave it back). We just loved it . . . until we began to run low on Bazooka bubblegum.

I didn't want anybody to get mine, so I hid my box under the bed. I would sneak out a piece or two every few days. Finally, when I got to the last six or eight pieces, I cut it into little bitty pieces. If anybody asked me for any, I'd just lie and say, "I haven't got any more." It was hidden under the bed. The last piece I saved for maybe a year. I mean, that piece of bubblegum was hard as a rock. Finally I thought, *I'm going to chew that. I'm gonna chew it now and have a little celebration, chew my bubblegum.* . . . Honey, it was like trying to chew a small portion of the Rock of Gibraltar. It was just hard as a rock. Blowing bubbles? Well, that was out of the question.

I just thought I was so generous when I had so much! But as soon as I began to run low on my supply, my generosity ran low.

Luci says we're very eager to give away and share with others things when we have ____ _____ of stuff—when we have a lot of one thing or we enjoy many things and we share with different people. That's fine. But when we _____ _____ , "don't be fooling with me, because I don't have anything to share."

Luci talked about sharing the fruit from her grapefruit tree—and her concern about sharing with the stranger who brought his son into her yard and started picking her grapefruit. Since that episode, she says, it has occurred to her that one of the most marvelous attributes about God is that he never _____ _____ ___ _____.

One of Luci's favorite things that God gives us is _____.

This is her favorite gift because:
 it forgives our _____
 it redeems us from _____
 it lifts us _____
 it puts our feet upon _____
 it permits us to _____
 it helps us in our _____
 it is sufficient for _____ _____ _____ __ _____.

> *The Lord is completely full of an unending supply of all the wonderful gifts that he has for us.*
>
> —*Luci*

Luci quotes an old hymn. Fill in the blanks as she quotes the words:

He giveth more grace when the _____ grows greater,
He sendeth more strength when the labors increase.
To added affliction he addeth his _____;
To multiplied trials, his multiplied peace.
When we have exhausted our store of _____,
When our _____ has failed ere the day is half done,
When we reach the end of our hoarded resources,
Our Father's full giving has only _____.
His love has no limit; his grace is no measure;
His power has no boundary known unto men.
For out of his _____ riches in Jesus,
He giveth, and giveth, and giveth again!

That, says Luci, is _____: giving and giving and giving and giving.

The song mentions "hoarding." Luci calls herself a "hoarder," a "pack rat."

Luci says that all of us hoard something. We're "tight" about something—really careful with it. We have only three things to spend while we're here. They are:

1. _____
2. _____
3. _____

> *I often say to the Lord, "Save me from myself!"*
>
> —*Luci*

Luci says that energy is no problem for her. She has lots. But money was a concern at one time. Her brother Chuck gave her this advice about tithing: You can never _____ God. You can never second-guess him. . . . Give *more* than _____. . . .

Luci's problem is with hoarding her _____. She says, "Do not _____ _____ on me. . . . Do not _____ _____ during *Law and Order* or *CSI*."

"Mrs. Greeley" thought Luci was an _____. But Luci thought she had acted more like a _____. "I wanted to do what I wanted to do with my time," she said.

> *You know what the joy of making money is? Giving it away! It's God's anyway!*
>
> *—Luci*

According to Luci, so often God sends things our way right in the middle of something we prefer to use in another way. We want _____ time, we want _____ arrangements, we want _____ plans, and God says, "_____. I'm going to do it _____ way. I'm never going to run out. I'm going to give you _____ _____ _____. And the best thing I'm going to give you is _____."

God gives us himself in the _____ of _____ _____.

He lives _____ us. That is our greatest reason to _____ a sensational life.

> *He came. He showed up. He moved in. And he still lives there. He will live there forever. He is my life. He is my light. He is the joy of my heart.*
>
> *He is my reason to celebrate.*
>
> *—Luci*

Luci talks about the birthday party she gave for Barbra Streisand's fortieth birthday. She and her friends had a great time, she said, but Barbra Streisand didn't show up. "She was too big for us," Luci said. "We just went right on celebrating without her there."

Years before that, Luci invited Jesus into her house, her heart—and he came.

Luci explains that a sensational life is taking the _____ of our lives and putting them back together in the person of Jesus Christ. That is sensationally living in celebration of his _____.

Luci provides this closing thought, a quote from the churchman Cardinal Newman posted on the wall of a museum in New Zealand:

> I will trust him, whatever, wherever I am. I can never be thrown away. If I am in sickness, my sickness may serve him. If I am in perplexity, my perplexity will serve him. If I am in sorrow, my sorrow will serve him. He does nothing in vain. He knows what he is about. He may take away my friends, he may throw me among strangers, he may make me feel desolate, make my spirit sink, hide my future from me, but he knows what he is about.

That, says Luci, is the sensational life. "I don't care what happens to you, what happens to me; he knows what he is about. He knows what he is about with your _____, your _____, your _____, with your _____, because he is God."

Taking It to Heart
Questions to help you personalize the lessons in the session

> **Leader's NOTES**
>
> Give the group a few minutes to work on these questions alone before you begin sharing. Encourage them to think about areas of life in which they tend to be hoarders.

1. Are you a pack rat, or do you know someone who is? What are some of the positives and negatives of being a pack rat?

   _____
   _____
   _____
   _____
   _____

2. Of the three things Luci mentioned—energy, money, and time—which is the easiest for you to give away? Why do you think that is?

   _____
   _____
   _____

3. Of those three things, which do you tend to hoard? Why?

   _____
   _____
   _____

4. Has there ever been a time when your hoarding of that resource got you into trouble or caused you to act in a "not-so-Christian" way? Describe.

   _____
   _____
   _____

Taking It Home
Questions to help you apply the lessons from the session

> ### Leader's **NOTES**
>
> Luci has shared some insightful stories as she bares her soul about some of the things that are part of her God-given personality—and how God is working to use her and teach her more about himself. Ask the group members not to focus on the negative; this is not meant to be a guilt-producing exercise. Each person will be in a different situation, so the women ought not compare themselves to each other but should think about how God might want them to not hoard any of the resources he has given them.

1. Consider the resource of energy. Where do you fall in that category at this point in your life? How are you using your energy to serve God?

   _____
   _____
   _____

2. Consider the resource of money. Where are you in that category? In what ways does God have control over your money? Is it a resource you use for him?

_____
_____
_____

3. Consider the resource of time. Where are you in that category at this point in your life? How do you use your time? Is it a resource that God knows is *his*?

_____
_____
_____

Back-Stage Pass—Bible Studies
Scripture passages used by Luci Swindoll

▶ Leader's **NOTES**

If you're following the Fast-Track Option, direct the women to skip to A Last Word at the end of the session and complete the Bible studies later, at their convenience. If your group is following the Full-Length Option, ask one of the women to read each passage aloud, then guide the women through the questions that follow.

1 Peter 1:1–5 (NIV)

¹Peter, an apostle of Jesus Christ, to God's elect, strangers in the world, scattered throughout Pontus, Galatia, Cappadocia, Asia and Bithynia, ²who have been chosen according to the foreknowledge of God the Father, through the sanctifying work of the Spirit, for obedience to Jesus Christ and sprinkling by his blood: Grace and peace be yours in abundance.

³Praise be to the God and Father of our Lord Jesus Christ! In his great mercy he has given us new birth into a living hope through the resurrection of Jesus Christ from the dead, ⁴and into an inheritance that can never perish, spoil or fade—kept in heaven for you, ⁵who through faith are shielded by God's power until the coming of the salvation that is ready to be revealed in the last time.

1 Peter 1:1–5 Study Questions

1. Luci makes it a point to quote 1 Peter 1:2—that Peter blesses his readers with "grace . . . in abundance." How would you define *grace*?

   _____
   _____
   _____

2. Why does Luci consider God's grace to be his greatest gift to us?

   _____
   _____
   _____

3. According to the verses above, what has God done for us because of his grace and mercy to us?

   _____
   _____
   _____

4. Beside the references below, write what each passage says about God's grace.
   John 1:16–17 _____
   Romans 3:22–24 _____
   Ephesians 2:8–9 _____
   Hebrews 4:16 _____

5. If you had to tell someone what God's grace means to you, what would you say?
___
___

Psalm 4:3, 6–8 (MSG)

Look at this: look
Who got picked by GOD!
He listens the split second I call to him. . . .

Why is everyone hungry for *more*? "More, more," they say.
"More, more."
I have God's more-than-enough,
More joy in one ordinary day

Than they get in all their shopping sprees.
At day's end I'm ready for sound sleep,
For you, GOD, have put my life back together.

Psalm 4:3, 6–8 Study Questions

1. Luci said a sensational life is taking the pieces of our lives and, as this psalm says, letting God put them back together. Are there some "pieces" of your life that aren't quite fitting into place right now? Explain.
___
___
___

2. Are you caught up in the desire to have "more" of something? If so, what is it? Why do you think it is so important to you?
___
___
___

3. Do you feel, like the psalmist, that you have "more joy in one ordinary day" than most other people have in the accumulation of "more stuff"? If not, why not?
   _____
   _____
   _____

4. David also wrote Psalm 16, which says, "You will teach me how to live a holy life. Being with you will fill me with joy; at your right hand I will find pleasure forever" (v. 11). It may not seem natural to find sensational joy in your ordinary days, but what, according to David, can make your life sensational and fill it with joy?
   _____
   _____
   _____

5. Think of one thing you can do each morning, before you get out of bed, to prepare yourself to find God's joy and to celebrate with him all day long.
   _____
   _____
   _____

A Last Word
An insight from this session to remember until next time

▷ Leader's **NOTES**

Luci closes the session with a focus on learning to trust God and celebrate with him how he can use every incident in our lives to glorify him. That is indeed something we can celebrate.

Closing Thought: Luci says that she wants to leave us with this thought, quoted from a little note on a wall beside a picture in a museum. Read it again as you end your session.

"I will trust him. Whatever, wherever I am, I can never be thrown away. If I am in sickness, my sickness will serve him. If I am in perplexity, my perplexity will serve him. If I am in sorrow, my sorrow will serve him. He does nothing in vain. He knows what he is about. He may take away my friends, he may throw me among strangers, he may make me feel desolate, make my spirit sink, hide my future from me—But he knows what he is about."

That is the sensational life. I don't care what happens to you, what happens to me; he knows what he is about. He knows what he is about with your money, with your energy, with your time, with your resources, because HE IS GOD!

> SESSION 8

WRAP-UP

SHEILA WALSH:
Sensational Little Gifts to Take Home

◉ Leader's NOTES

Like the Introductory Session, the Wrap-Up Session is intentionally unscripted so you can use the allotted time in the way that works best for you or your group.

Before the session begins, cue Tape 3 to Sheila's thirteen-minute wrap-up message and the conference closing.

Open the session with prayer, thanking God for the time you've spent together and the opportunity to learn how God wants you to live truly sensational lives. Have participants read aloud the portion of John 10:10 as quoted below from several different translations.

New Revised Standard Version
"I came that they may have life, and have it abundantly."

New International Version
"I have come that they may have life, and have it to the full."

New Living Translation

"My purpose is to give life in all its fullness."

The Message

"I came so they can have real and eternal life, more and better life than they ever dreamed of."

Next, play Sheila's Wrap-Up message from Tape 3. Encourage the group members to take notes on the lines below. Play the tape all the way through to the end, including the singing of the Women of Faith theme song and the other closing elements.

Use the remainder of the time to share what you've learned during these sessions. Go through the sessions one by one, inviting participants to review their notes and briefly share interesting insights they've gained. You might say, "Let's go back and quickly review our notes and then share some of the highlights of these sessions. We'll begin with Sheila's message on vision in a sensational life. As you look back through your notes on this message, tell us one favorite truth you learned or one change you made in your life because of something you discovered during this session. Be sure to look through your notes on the Bible studies as well as Sheila's message."

Ask the group members to remember that at the beginning of the series they discussed what sensational living meant to them. Ask each woman how her perception of that kind of life has changed. Then ask which of the "little gifts" from the speakers will be most useful as reminders of sensational living in their own lives.

Sharing the Blessings

What are the little gifts the speakers have sent you as mementos of this series?

Sheila's gift: a pair of _____ _____

It reminds you that we are in a _____ _____. Whether you've just begun to run the race or whether you find yourself _____ on the track, weighed down by the *why?* questions, or asking, "Lord, in the middle of all of this, how can I finish well?" Remember what the writer to the Hebrews said: "Study how Jesus did it. He never lost sight of where he was going." So whatever is happening in your life, joys or sorrows, put on your running shoes, and run to God.

Patsy's gift: _____

You realize it's a ____ _____ _____ _____. You can see all the ways the path has twisted and turned. You remember tear-soaked days, bitter times, hard times. You see other times where there was tremendous joy, and you remember the laughter. . . . The one thing you will notice . . . is that in every single place, God is there. . . . And what a wonderful word from Patsy to each one of us to learn . . . to learn to keep silent and to let God fight the battle.

Thelma's gift: _____

On it is all _____ information. . . . Thelma's message reminds us . . . of a simple, profound, life-changing sensational fact: God is ___ _____. . . . He knew every day that you will live before you were even in your mother's womb. That's why in these days of turmoil . . . we can have a confidence, knowing that Jesus is in control. We can know peace in the midst of the most turbulent times if we remember, "Be anxious for _____."

Barbara's gift: _____

Into the well-watered soil of your broken heart he will plants seeds of _____. And when we hope in him, we will not ever be disappointed.

Marilyn's gift: _____

In the window you notice a little sign that says, "Available to those who need a _____ _____, a _____ _____, or a _____ _____." Just as Luci would not let her beloved friend take that hazardous trip by herself, . . . the God of the universe is the same with you. Jesus will not let you go one mile without him.

Luci's gift: _____, the very last one from the tree.

Jesus says to you, "May I have that? . . . . I want it all: your time, your energy, your money, your hopes and dreams, your family. Give it all to me." When we put everything we've hoarded into the hands of Jesus, when we become that little boy who gives his lunch to Jesus, he blesses it and breaks it and feeds the multitudes, your life, your *stuff*, is safe in his hands. If we leave here remembering to stand in the gap for one another and to say to him, "I surrender all," truly we will live a sensational life.

Close with a prayer, asking God to remind you daily that you are indeed living a sensational life because you have a sensational Savior!

Featured Speakers

PATSY CLAIRMONT
MARILYN MEBERG
LUCI SWINDOLL
SHEILA WALSH
THELMA WELLS

"NO EYE HAS SEEN, NO EAR HAS HEARD, NO MIND HAS CONCEIVED WHAT GOD HAS PREPARED FOR THOSE WHO LOVE HIM." *I Corinthians 2:9*

THOUSANDS OF WOMEN ARE GATHERING FOR A LIFE-CHANGING EXPERIENCE.

The Great Adventure Tour 2003

The Great Adventure 2003 Dates*

February 21–22
Sacramento, CA
ARCO Arena

March 14–15
Memphis, TN
Pyramid Arena

March 28–29
Columbus, OH
Nationwide Arena

April 4–5
Kansas City, MO
Kemper Arena

May 2–3
Shreveport, LA
CenturyTel Center

May 16–17
Louisville, KY
Kentucky Fair & Expo Ctr

May 30–31
Billings, MT
MetraPark

June 6–7
Anaheim, CA
Arrowhead Pond

June 13–14
Charleston, SC
N. Charleston Coliseum

June 20–21
Ft. Lauderdale, FL
Office Depot Center

June 27–28
Washington, DC
MCI Center

July 11–12
Dallas, TX
America Airlines Ctr

July 18–19
Toronto/Hamilton, ON
Copps Coliseum

July 25–26
Denver, CO
Pepsi Center

August 1–2
Atlanta, GA
Philips Arena

August 8–9
Oklahoma City, OK
Ford Center

August 15–16
Ames, IA
Hilton Coliseum

August 22–23
Chicago, IL
United Center

September 5–6
Anaheim, CA
Arrowhead Pond

September 12–13
St. Paul, MN
Xcel Energy Center

September 19–20
Albany, NY
Pepsi Arena

September 26–27
Detroit, MI
Palace of Auburn Hills

October 3–4
Hartford, CT
Hartford Civic Center

October 10–11
Portland, OR
Rose Garden Arena

October 17–18
Vancouver, BC
General Motors Place

October 24–25
Charlotte, NC
Charlotte Coliseum

October 31–November 1
Omaha, NE
Omaha Conv Ctr & Arena

November 7–8
Philadelphia, PA
First Union Center

November 14–15
Orlando, FL
TD Waterhouse Centre

*Dates and locations subject to change.

WOMEN OF FAITH®
A Division of Thomas Nelson, Inc.

For more information call **1-888-49-FAITH**
or visit us on the web at **womenoffaith.com**